HANGED IN LANCASHIRE

TRUE CRIME FROM WHARNCLIFFE
Foul Deeds and Suspicious Deaths Series

OTHER TRUE CRIME BOOKS FROM WHARNCLIFFE

Please contact us via any of the methods below for more information or a catalogue.

WHARNCLIFFE BOOKS
47 Church Street – Barnsley – South Yorkshire – S70 2AS
Tel: 01226 734555 – 734222 Fax: 01226 734438
E-mail: enquiries@pen-and-sword.co.uk
Website: www.wharncliffebooks.co.uk

Hanged In

LANCASHIRE

MARTIN BAGGOLEY

First published in Great Britain in 2010 by
Wharncliffe Local History
an imprint of
Pen & Sword Books Ltd
47 Church Street
Barnsley
South Yorkshire
S70 2AS

ISBN 978 1 84563 100 0

A CIP catalogue record for this book is available from the
British Library.

Typeset in 11/13pt Plantin by
Mac Style, Beverley, East Yorkshire

Printed and bound in the UK by
CPI Antony Rowe, Chippenham, Wiltshire

Pen & Sword Books Ltd incorporates the imprints of Pen & Sword
Aviation, Pen & Sword Maritime, Pen & Sword Military,
Wharncliffe Local History, Pen and Sword Select, Pen and Sword
Military Classics and Leo Cooper.

For a complete list of Pen & Sword titles please contact
PEN & SWORD BOOKS LIMITED
47 Church Street, Barnsley, South Yorkshire, S70 2AS, England
E-mail: enquiries@pen-and-sword.co.uk
Website: www.pen-and-sword.co.uk

Contents

Introduction

Lancaster, for centuries the county's only assize town, had long been the setting for most of Lancashire's executions. The castle served as the court at which all of the most serious crimes were dealt with and it was outside its walls that those sentenced to death were hanged. This account begins in the late eighteenth century, the age of the Bloody Code, when there were numerous capital offences and mass public executions, which were often carried out in front of crowds of many thousands. It ends 170 years later with the simultaneous executions of the last two men to be put to death before the abolition of the death penalty. In the intervening years, more than 400 men and women died at the end of the rope in a number of different locations across the county and for a wide range of crimes.

The first cases described are of a burglar and croft-breaker who were executed not at Lancaster but on Kersal Moor and Newton Heath, close to the scenes of their crimes. These were intended to act as a warning to anyone in those districts thinking of committing similar deeds. This had been common practice in the past, but by the close of the eighteenth century such events were becoming increasingly rare, and indeed these were the last executions carried out in these circumstances in the county. Crimes other than murder, which are also discussed, include highway robbery, forgery and sodomy. The early years of the nineteenth century were marked by much unrest and Lancashire witnessed serious Luddite riots; a chapter is devoted to these disturbances and the subsequent executions of some of the participants.

As the nineteenth century progressed it was becoming clear that Lancaster could no longer cope alone with the increasing demands being placed on the criminal justice system. Therefore, in 1835, Liverpool became an assize town which meant that serious cases were heard there and executions began to take place at the Kirkdale House of Correction, and later at Walton Gaol. In 1864, Manchester was also created an assize town but the proposed new county gaol at Strangeways was not built, leading to several executions being carried out before the walls of the New Bailey in Salford. By the time Strangeways opened its gates in 1868, executions had ceased to be public spectacles, and henceforth those convicted of murder, by now the only capital crime except for one or two rare exceptions, were dispatched in private.

In 1912 the last execution took place at Knutsford Gaol in Cheshire and afterwards murderers convicted in that county would be hanged in neighbouring Lancashire, which has led to a chapter being devoted to a murder committed in Cheshire. All of the county's hanging gaols are represented and murders from across the county are included.

The book spans more than two centuries, and the executed range from rioters driven by fear of the future to the callous mother who poisoned a loving and trusting daughter for financial gain. I also discuss possible miscarriages of justice and the question of insanity to reflect the controversy that has always surrounded capital punishment.

Acknowledgements
I am grateful for the assistance given to me in the research and writing of this book by the staff at Manchester Central Library and Liverpool Central Library.

CHAPTER 1

To Deter Others
1790 & 1798

For several centuries, Lancaster was Lancashire's only assize town. Its ancient castle was the location of all trials involving serious crimes, and as many of those were punishable by death, the town was the site of almost all of the county's executions. However, this account of hangings in the county begins with two exceptions to this rule, which took place towards the close of the eighteenth century, when the country was still in the grip of the Bloody Code.

It was late on the night of Sunday 17 January 1790, when Thomas Cheetham, landlord of the *Dog and Partridge* on Stretford Road, Manchester secured the premises and retired to bed with his wife. He had just blown out the bedside candle when the Cheethams heard what they recognised as the sound of the back door to the inn being forced open. Seconds later five men, all of whom had blackened faces to disguise their identities, burst into the terrified couple's room.

After binding Mr and Mrs Cheetham, one of the intruders removed a ring forcibly from Mrs Cheetham's finger. However, she begged the man not to take it as it was her wedding ring. Surprisingly he relented and returned the ring to her finger. The gang remained in the house for more than ninety minutes during which time they subjected the couple to various threats of violence. When they eventually left they took with them Mr Cheetham's watch, £8 in cash, a number of silver spoons, a quantity of linen, clothes and several bottles of brandy.

This had been the latest in a spate of similarly violent burglaries in the district, and although there had been no fatal incidents, the authorities made a determined effort to catch the one gang believed to be responsible for all of the crimes.

Details of the break in at the *Dog and Partridge* were circulated throughout the North West, and in early February two men suspected of being involved in the robberies were arrested in Liverpool. One escaped, but the other, James McNamara, on whom items of property belonging to the Cheethams were found, was returned to Manchester, where on 10 February, he

1798

A full true and particular Account of the Trial of

JAMES M'NAMARA,

Who is to be executed on KERSAL MOOR, on Saturday se'nnight, for a Burglary, in the House of Mr. Cheetham, the Dog and Partridge, near Manchester.

DURING his trial before my Lord Judge, he behaved in a most infolent manner, much to the aftonifhment of a crouded Court; but fince is Condemnation, he has been much humbled by his awful fentence.

He has been an old offender, and is fuppofed was a confederate of the two unfortunate men, who fuffered at Liverpool, for Houfe breaking, at St. Ann's, Richmond, near the place.

During his trial a number of witneffes were examined which gave every particular as to his perfon, and property which he had found upon him when apprehended.

He his a ftout broad fet man, about thirty years of age, and of a moft daring countenance.

After he was found guilty, the Judge paffed fentence of death upon him, and entreated him to prepare himfelf for the fatal day, as the crime for which he was going to fuffer for, had been made a moft daring practice of about the neighbourhood which he would fhortly meet the fatal day, which it is hoped will be a warning to others, who has not the fear of God before their eyes.

The prifoner then made fome very infolent replies to his Lordfhip, which furprifed every fpectator.

WHEN rifing from the bed of death,
O'erwhelm'd with guilt and fear;
I fee my Maker face to face,
O how fhall I appear.
If, while pardon may be found,
And mercy may be fought;
My heart with inward horror fhrinks,
And trembling at the thought.
When thou, O Lord, fhall ftand difclos'd,
In Majefty ferve,
And fit in judgment on my foul,
O how fhall I appear,

But thou haft told the troubled mind,
Who does her fins lament;
The timely tribute of her tears;
Shllendlefs woe prevent.
Then fee the forrow of my heart,
Ere yet it be too late,
And hear my Saviour's dying groans,
To give my forrows weight.
For never fhall my foul defpair,
Her pardon to procure;
Who knows thy only Son has died,
To make her pardon fure.

A broadside published following the trial of James McNamara. Manchester Central Library

was committed to stand trial at the Lancaster Assizes. After spending six months in the castle, he stood his trial in August.

When McNamara's trial opened, details of his criminal background were given to the jury together with details of the possessions stolen at the break in at the *Dog and Partridge* which were found in his possession. It took very little time for McNamara to be found guilty, and he returned to his cell having been sentenced to death and having been told by the judge that he should not expect to be shown mercy.

The condemned man was thirty-two years old, and had been born and spent his formative years in Dromcondra, near Dublin. His parents, who had a small dairy farm, were honest and hard working, and had managed to provide their son with a good education, which unfortunately, he failed to take advantage of. He travelled to Dublin regularly to sell the farm's produce, and when still in his teens fell into bad company. Whilst still living in Ireland, he was convicted of several crimes and was eventually sentenced to death, but was reprieved and instead was sentenced to be transported to North America.

However, when his ship put into St John's, Newfoundland, he escaped. Unable to return home, where he would be recognised, he made his way to England. He settled in Manchester, where initially he worked as a labourer, but he soon returned to his criminal ways.

McNamara would no doubt be expecting to be hanged outside the walls of Lancaster Castle. However, it was decided that he should be executed in Manchester, with the intention of deterring others who might be thinking of committing similar crimes in that town. The execution was to be witnessed by as large a crowd as possible, and it was decided that McNamara would die on the hill on Kersal Moor, one of the highest natural points in the district. Thus, on Thursday 9 September, the condemned man was taken by carriage from Lancaster to the New Bailey Gaol in Salford, where he spent the final two days of his life.

To ensure that as many local people as possible witnessed McNamara's degrading final hours, it was decided that he would not be taken directly to the gallows. On the morning of his execution he was shackled and placed in a small cart, which formed part of a grand procession, which was driven through the streets of Manchester and Salford for more than two hours. Marching in front of the cart were four sheriff's officers and eight javelin men. Two of the former and four of the latter walked at each side of the cart, immediately behind which were another eight javelin men and four sheriff's officers. They were followed by the Under Sheriff and a number of local clergymen. Next came a coach carrying many of the local magistrates, and at the rear of the procession came the Deputy Constable, the boroughreeves and constables of the two towns, the beadles, all of whom were wearing their distinctive cloaks and caps, and a number of special constables. As this impressive sight made its way to Kersal Moor, all of the local church bells rang out.

Several thousand spectators had assembled at the execution site and a penitent McNamara, who had now lost the arrogance he had displayed at his trial, addressed the crowd for a few minutes. He spoke of the justness of his sentence, exhorted those present to avoid bad company and minutes later he died without a struggle.

There were no crowd problems, but the event was marred by the activities of a pickpocket, who although seen in the act, managed to make his escape, which given the massive turnout of the area's forces of law and order was rather ironic.

Eight years later, on Saturday 15 September 1798, following a respite of seven days granted by the Duke of Portland to await the sentencing judge's views on a plea for a reprieve, twenty-two-year-old George Russell was hanged on Newton Heath, Manchester. He had been convicted of croft-breaking on 5 June, when he stole cloth, velveteen and Genoa cord valued at £20, the property of Thomas Shorrocks, a local dyer and bleacher.

At this time there was no formal means of appealing against conviction or sentence, but it was open to individuals to make representations on behalf of the condemned by writing to the Secretary of State, who might then consult the trial judge. One petition was submitted on Russell's behalf and that was from his mother, Ann Russell. He was the youngest of her six sons,

The laſt dying Speech and Confeſſion of

GEORGE RUSSELL,

22 Years of Age, born in the County of Armagh, in Ireland,

Who was executed at Newton Heath, on Saturday Sept. 15, 1798,

For Croft Breaking, at Mancheſter.

I *GEORGE RUSSELL*, now under the Sentence of Death, publiſh this my laſt dying Speech and Confeſſion, with an earneſt deſire that others may be warned by my example.

I acknowledge myſelf guilty of the crime for which I ſtand condemned, I deſerve to ſuffer the ſentence, and pray God to have mercy upon my ſoul for Chriſt's ſake.

Sabbath-breaking and bad company were the introduction to my ſin and my miſery; Bad women eſpecially, have been the cauſe of my ruin, many of them live by plunder themſelves, they occaſion poor young men to make uſe of improper methods of gaining money to give to them, and I verily believe that they are the cauſe of bringing almoſt every one to the gallows who come thither; It would have been well for me if I had never ſeen one of them, and, as a dying man, I warn others to beware of them.

I ſincerely forgive those who have been concerned in my proſecution, and have nobody to blame but myſelf. God be merciful to me a Sinner.

His
George ✕ Russell,
Mark.

A broadside describing George Russell's execution. Manchester Central Library

all of whom had served in the armed services, and he had served in the Royal Navy. She wrote of his previous good character and that he had acted out of character as he had been drunk when he committed the crime.

In his response the judge noted that in the previous twelve months, Mr Shorrocks had lost material from his croft to the value of more than £500, and croft-breaking was a crime now reaching a 'very alarming height' in the district. The judge was unmoved by Mrs Russell's letter and recommended that mercy was not shown in this case. As a result there was no reprieve and the authorities believed that this was an appropriate case for the execution to be carried out close to the scene of the crime and be used as a deterrent to those in the area who might be considering committing a similar offence. It was therefore decided that it would take place not in Lancaster but on Newton Heath, Manchester.

At ten o'clock on the morning of the execution, Russell was placed on an elevated seat in a cart so that he was visible to the many thousands of spectators who lined the route from the New Bailey Gaol to the Heath. This was followed by a mourning coach carrying the Reverends Mr Cheek, Dr Bayley and Mr Robey. The boroughreeves and constables from Manchester and Salford marched alongside.

Later, as he waited for the cart to be drawn from underneath him, Russell called on those who had gathered to witness his death to avoid sabbath-breaking, improper female company and keeping low company in public houses. After acknowledging the justness of his sentence and expressing contrition, he prayed in silence for a few moments before the cart moved forward.

This would prove to be the last occasion on which an execution would occur in any place other than Lancaster, or later in the nineteenth century, in one of the other assize towns which would be created in the county.

CHAPTER 2

A Highway Robbery
1803

J oseph Jones, a wool manufacturer of Rochdale, also acted as agent in the North West of England for James Bell of Uttoxeter. James travelled north to meet with Joseph at his home on Monday 14 November 1803. The two men agreed that on the following day, Joseph would ride the twelve miles to Manchester to conduct some business on behalf of his client.

On Tuesday, Joseph did not conclude his business until six o'clock in the evening and it was already dark when he left Manchester on the return journey to Rochdale. He was accompanied by a friend, Mr Burgess, who was riding a short distance ahead. They had travelled about four miles, when a man stepped out into the road and grabbed the bridle of Joseph's horse, causing it to stop. The man produced a blunderbuss, which had a bayonet attached to the end, and demanded that Joseph 'Deliver or you are a dead man in a moment'. Mr Burgess heard the commotion and came to a stop but as he did so the robber shouted: 'If you come any nearer I'll shoot you too'. Fearing for his life, Mr Burgess galloped away from the scene.

The robber again turned to Joseph, saying: 'Look sharp or I'll run you through. Deliver or you are a dead man'. Joseph pleaded to him, saying: 'Spare my life and I'll give you all that I have, but I do not have much money'. From his breeches, he pulled a purse, which contained several bank notes, but the highwayman was not satisfied with this and searched him. He took a penknife and some copper coins from Joseph's waistband pocket; from his other pockets he took several silver and gold coins and a letter, which had been written and signed by James Bell, authorising Joseph to conduct business on his behalf in Manchester on that day. The robber was still not convinced that he had all of his victim's valuables, for he screamed: 'Damn your blood, you must have a watch'. Joseph insisted that he did not have one, and after a fruitless search lasting two or three more minutes, the robber ran from the scene.

Mr Burgess had not deserted his friend, for a few minutes later he returned with a group of men. However, it was now too dark for them to make a search of the area and they returned to Manchester, where the crime was reported to Joseph Nadin, the town's Deputy Constable.

Nadin, accompanied by several armed colleagues, were soon riding towards the scene of the crime. He treated this with great urgency for in the very recent past two men had been shot to death in the same area during a similar highway robbery. It was by now ten o'clock at night, and after travelling only a short distance from the town, the officers encountered a man fitting the description of the robber, given by Joseph. The Deputy Constable detained the suspect, who had initially believed he was the victim of a gang of robbers. When the true identities of the men were revealed, the Deputy thought the man looked even more terrified than when he had believed them to be villains.

Joseph Nadin. Manchester Central Library

The suspect turned out to be twenty-three-year-old Joseph Brown, who told Nadin that he had walked to Manchester from Bury, where he lived. He was searched and was found to be carrying an unloaded pistol, a penknife which fitted the description given by Joseph of his own that had been stolen, a pocket book containing three guineas and an Irish Bank £10 banknote. Three pawn tickets, two of which were for gold watches and the other for a silver watch, were also found, together with a bloodstained shirt which had been carefully folded and which the prisoner had attempted to conceal in his hat. However, it was the discovery of the letter signed by James Bell that had been given to Joseph and which the robber had stolen, that provided a direct link to the robbery.

Brown was held in Lancaster Castle as he awaited his trial at the Assizes of April 1804, when he appeared before Judge Alan de Chambre, charged with highway robbery, to which he pleaded not guilty. The trial was relatively brief, and apart from the identification evidence provided by the victim, the testimony of two other witnesses proved to be particularly damning. James Bell identified the letter found in the accused's possession, as that which he had given to Joseph on the eve of the crime. James Richardson, a Manchester cutler, identified Brown as the man who had visited his shop on the morning of 15 November 1803 and who bought the blunderbuss, bayonet and pistol, which had been found on Brown by the Deputy Constable, and for which he had paid two and a half guineas. No witnesses were called on behalf of the man in the dock, and the jury took just a few minutes to find him guilty, after which he was sentenced to death.

Brown's execution was fixed for Saturday 28 April, but he advised Reverend Richard Withnell, Chaplain of Lancaster Gaol, he thought that although not charged with the crimes, his death sentence had been imposed because the judge believed he had been responsible for the earlier murders of the two men on the road between Manchester and Rochdale. However, he could provide an alibi for the time the murders had been committed, and another witness could be provided to explain how his shirt came to be smeared in blood.

The chaplain wrote to members of the condemned man's family in Penrith, on 19 April, and in a letter to his brother-in-law, stonemason Samuel Bell, he included the following information:

> He has declared to me repeatedly, upon the word of a dying man, that he was in Ireland, a sergeant in a Volunteer Regiment, when the men were found; that he can prove his being in Dublin at that time, as well as his good and regular contact from the testimony of his officers and other respectable characters there, and he would have done so upon his trial had he known that he was so strongly suspected. Indeed, I am inclined to think that he would not have been left for execution if that had not rested upon him.

Reverend Withnell also addressed the issue of the bloodstains on his clothing:

> He says it was occasioned by a hurt he received on his hand in his passage from Dublin to Liverpool, that it bled upon his coat when he laid his arm upon it; that Captain Jones, now at Liverpool, saw the coat when he was on board his vessel; knows that the blood came upon it in that way, and upon that particular part. If these circumstances can be brought forward in a proper manner by his friends, perhaps something may yet be done; but as I said before, all depends upon expedition in getting the respite.

Meanwhile, the condemned's mother, Mary Brown, wrote to Lord Viscount Lowther urging that he act on her behalf and use his influence to arrange for her son's execution to be postponed:

> I have now to request of your Lordship to make application to the Secretary of State for a respite till further enquiry may be made into his former conduct. I hope your Lordship will pardon the boldness I have taken in making this request of your Lordship and if such desire can be granted, it will relieve the distress of an affectionate mother.

A letter written by Brown's mother, Margaret, to Lord Viscount Lowther seeking his support in seeking a respite. The National Archives

Brown's family was successful in gaining a respite, but it was for seven days only. John Higgins, the Keeper of Lancaster Gaol, wrote to the office of the Secretary of State to acknowledge receipt of details of the respite, but added that he had advised the prisoner that there 'was not the slightest hope for success in his application'. Indeed, it proved impossible for any new evidence to be presented in the time allowed the family, and Brown's fate was probably sealed in the trial judge's letter of 28 April to the Secretary of State, in which he commented:

The fact that two men who had been shot having been found upon the road near Manchester some time ago, stated in the letters sent in support of the application on behalf of the prisoner, was not in evidence, and probably the prisoner may be free from imputation in respect of the murder of these men. But forming my opinion on the circumstances that were in evidence and having no evidence respecting the former character and conduct of the prisoner, I thought it my duty to leave the law to take its course.

And the law did take its course, for Joseph Brown was hanged outside Lancaster Castle on 5 May 1804.

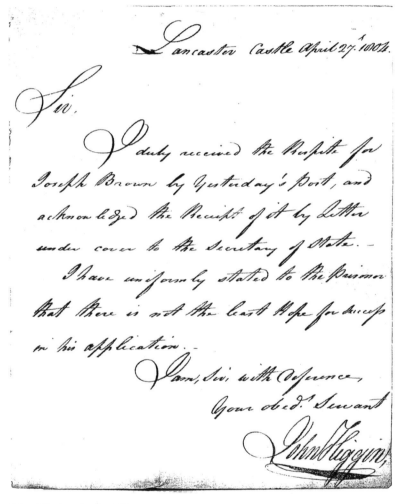

John Higgins, Gaoler of Lancaster, wrote to the Secretary of State to acknowledge receipt of the respite for Brown, but adds that he has warned the prisoner not to expect a reprieve. The National Archives

CHAPTER 3

The Manchester Forgers
1804

Acting on information provided by grocer Thomas Warburton, constables William Knowles and Timothy Browning entered the *Unicorn Inn* at Altrincham on the evening of 3 April 1804. Thomas had reported receiving what he believed to be a forged Bank of England one pound note from a man now drinking at the inn. He pointed the man out, who was detained and who identified himself as James Murphy. He was searched and another four one pound notes were found on him, which it was suspected were also forgeries and which Constable Knowles initialled before escorting the prisoner to the lock up.

Murphy, an Irish-born soldier who had enlisted nine years earlier in Ireland under the assumed name of Doyle, clearly recognised the very serious position he was in and that he faced possible execution for the crime of *uttering*, a crime concerned in putting into circulation documents, including banknotes and bills of exchange, knowing them to be forged. His offer to provide details of his associates and the whereabouts of the equipment used and to be a witness for the Crown was accepted, and he was granted immunity from prosecution. As he would later admit under cross-examination at the assizes, he was giving evidence against his former associates solely to save himself.

Murphy named the forgers of the notes in his possession as being John Ogilvey, an engraver by trade and Thomas Smith, both of whom lived in the centre of Manchester, where he claimed to have met them in July of the previous year. He claimed, however, that it was not until several months later that he learnt of their plans to forge Bank of England notes, and he agreed to help them pass the notes into circulation. He had visited both their homes and was able to advise the authorities where the equipment and materials used to produce the forgeries were hidden, much of it being in Smith's house.

He had met the two men in the *Crown and Anchor* in Manchester earlier that day, before travelling to Altrincham. They had handed him seven forged one pound notes for which he agreed to pay them three half-guineas, once he had spent them and had the money with which to pay the pair. In Altrincham, he had used three of the notes to buy food and drink, but he had not been able to hoodwink Thomas Warburton.

The information provided by Murphy was sufficient for Thomas Warburton, being the main prosecutor, to obtain warrants from a Manchester magistrate, enabling the homes of the alleged forgers to be searched. Thus, on the evening of 4 April at ten o'clock, simultaneous raids were carried out. Thomas Warburton, who was accompanied by constables Peter Whitehead, Robert Potter and George Gyte, called at Smith's house on Spear Street, while constables Green and John Ridley visited the home of Ogilvey on Minshull Street.

Smith's house was in darkness and with a lighted candle the constables gained entry, rushing upstairs, where they found Smith and his wife asleep. The aggrieved grocer had not met Smith, but confirmed that he fitted the description given the previous day by Murphy. Smith was handcuffed and asked his wife for a glass of water. As she handed it to him, he slowly shook his head as though he already realised what his fate would be.

The property was just as Murphy had described and there was no difficulty in locating the places where the materials and equipment were hidden. Smith refused to hand over a key to a downstairs back room, so Thomas kicked it open. In the room he and the constables found a printing press, paper which had been cut into the shape and size of bank notes together with a large quantity of ink. Constable Gyte lifted a loose flagstone in the floor, which Murphy had told them about, and underneath were the plates used to produce the forgeries.

Meanwhile, constables Green and Ridley visited Ogilvey's house and were admitted by the elderly woman with whom the alleged forger and his wife lodged. He and his wife were asleep in their room, and the surprised Ogilvey was pulled from the bed and a search made of his breeches and waistcoat which were draped over a chair. Constable Ridley found a folded banknote in one of the pockets, and as he unfolded it, Ogilvey's wife jumped from the bed, blew the constable's candle out, and grabbed at the note. She ripped a piece from it, but the constable managed to hold on to most of it. The smaller piece was recovered from his wife and both pieces were initialled by Constable Ridley. It was evident that Ogilvey's wife appreciated the very serious implications for her husband of the discovery of the undoubtedly forged bank note. A search of the premises led to the discovery of paper and materials for use in forging bank notes.

The following day, at the New Bailey Gaol, Ogilvey was interviewed by James Taylor, one of Manchester's beadles. The prisoner admitted that he, Smith and Murphy had been planning to print many more banknotes than the seven they had produced so far. The note found in his breeches was to be given to Murphy to dispose of, and they had planned to print at least another 100 in the following few days. At the close of the interview, Ogilvey asked Taylor what he thought would happen to him, to which the beadle replied that he would probably be hanged. On hearing this, Ogilvey cried out: 'For God's sake, don't let me be hanged, let me be transported for life. I'll never be seen in the country again.'

When Ogilvey and Smith came to trial, they were charged with forging just one Bank of England note. Evidence was given by Thomas Warburton, the beadle, and the constables who had been concerned in the case, but the most damming testimony of all was that given by Murphy, who had clearly been much more deeply involved than he admitted.

There were two other important witnesses for the Crown: Garnett Terry, an engraver employed by the Bank of England, and Thomas Glover, the bank's Inspector of Banknotes. Their evidence confirmed that the plates found at Smith's house had been used to print all of the forgeries so far discovered, and they drew particular attention to the poor quality of the forged signature of the bank official used on the notes.

Smith and Ogilvey were men of previous good character and a number of character witnesses appeared on their behalf. Nevertheless, they were convicted and sentenced to death by the trial judge, Sir Alan de Chambre. At the conclusion of the assizes the judge wrote to the Secretary of State in London, detailing his concern that thirteen men had appeared before him at the assizes charged with uttering, forgery or being in possession of a forged banknote. Such crimes, he felt were prevalent in the county and he believed that deterrent sentences were necessary. He had sentenced seven men to death, namely Smith and Ogilvey together with Michael Hughes, John McGee, Thomas Boadle, and brothers James and Joseph Bridge.

However, John Higgins, Governor of Lancaster Gaol and the chaplain, Joseph Rowley, wrote to the judge asking him to consider leniency, and in their letter of 30 August they made the following observations:

It is a melancholy reflection that so many lives are to be taken for similar offences. You no doubt deeply lament that there should be a necessity for this profusion of blood. You must with others shudder at the dreadful catastrophe; seven immortal beings to be launched into eternity before the awful tribunal of the Supreme Being to answer for the deeds during their existence on earth.

They continued by suggesting that some of the condemned were perhaps less culpable than others, and they could be shown mercy:

Michael Hughes has been merely the instrument of a more designing man, H Hamilton, who fortunately for him, escaped the hand of Justice. The younger of the Bridges has not the cunning nor the learning of his elder brother. He in all probability was prevailed upon to enter into his brother's schemes, without reflecting upon the fatal consequences. Boadle's injudicious and open conduct, particularly during his trial, cannot have escaped the notice of the Bank Solicitors; and Ogilvey's tender age and the distressed

Lancaster Castle Aug. 24 1804

Sir,

Herewith I send a marked Calendar, agreeably to your request.

The Judge has left seven unhappy men under sentence of Death for forging and uttering forged Bank of England Notes. Viz.

"John Ogilvey, Thomas Smith, Michael "Hughes, Thomas Boadle, James Bridge, "Joseph Bridge and John Bradshaw Magee."

The usual time of Execution will be on Saturday the eighth day of September at Noon. —

I am, with great deference,
Your most Obedient
humble Servant

John Higgins

John King, Esq.
Under Secretary of State &c.

In this letter John Higgins advised the Secretary of State of the names of those condemned to death at the Assizes. The National Archives

The humble petition of Margaret Ogilvey
To the Honourable Mr Justice Chambre.

May it please your Lordship,

    To permit me in the distress of my heart to plead with your Lordship for a mitigation of punishment to my poor unfortunate husband John Ogilvey, in consideration of his extreme youth — not yet eighteen; the candid confession he made of this his first offence; and that no injury has been sustained to the public from the fatal crime into which his inexperience has been betrayed by evil counsellors.

    Permit me to hope that there is a possibility of his life being spared, by means of the compassion, which in your Lordship has been ever known to plead for the unfortunate through your merciful administration of justice.

    And the life so spared will

John Ogilvey's wife, Margaret, wrote this letter pleading for leniency for her husband. The National Archives

I trust be devoted to the good of his
fellow creatures; and in fervent prayer
for your Lordships, in which will most
gratefully join,

    My Lord,

        Your Lordships'

           humble & afflicted petitioner

Lancaster
August 19. 1804.
                Margret Ogilvie

condition of his relatives, plead strongly on his behalf. This youth has become the victim of an artful man, Murphy, a man perhaps unparalleled in seduction, who, we understand, is deeply connected in forgeries of this description, and who bought the plate in Dublin.

Relatives of the condemned also attempted to intercede on their behalf, one of whom was John Bridge, cousin of the Bridge brothers, who wrote to the King from his home in Rochdale, part of which noted:

The truth is their crime was the effect of bad advice and the indiscretion of the moment, not of any rooted baseness or depravity of heart. They are lovely grateful youths, and would, no doubt, if pardoned, become worthy members of society and worthy subjects.

Ogilvey's father, John and the condemned's wife, Margaret, wrote to Sir Alan de Chambre, seeking a reprieve. Part of his wife's letter read as follows:

May it please your Lordship, to permit me in the distress of my heart to plead with your Lordship for mitigation of punishment to my poor unfortunate husband John Ogilvey, in consideration of his extreme youth, not yet eighteen, the candid confession he made of this his first offence, and that no injury has been sustained to the public from the fatal crime in which his inexperience has been betrayed by his evil counsellors.

The Secretary of State sought the views of the governor and directors of the Bank of England in Ogilvey's case. They replied that they had no objection to mercy being extended to him, and commented:

The youth of the prisoner perhaps may be one of the strongest pleas in favour of mitigation of his punishment to transportation, all which they submit to His Majesty's Ministers.

Shortly before the executions were scheduled to take place, Michael Hughes and Joseph Bridge learnt that they were to be reprieved. The others, John Ogilvey, Thomas Smith, John McGee, Thomas Boadle and James Bridge died together outside the walls of Lancaster Castle on 8 September 1804.

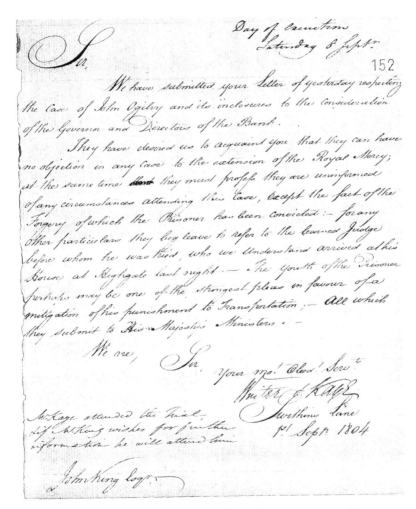

A letter from the Bank of England confirming the Directors had no objection to a reprieve for John Ogilvey. The National Archives

CHAPTER 4

The Warrington Sodomites 1806

In early May 1806, Warrington's Volunteers were called out to assist with the arrests of more than twenty local men who were suspected of being involved in homosexual practices. They were said to have met regularly at a public house in Sankey and in the homes of some of the town's leading residents, and at these meetings had called each other 'brother'. A number of trials followed at the Lancaster Assizes later that year, which would result in the executions of five men. In view of the offences and the nature of the evidence given, judges often ordered that written notes taken during the hearing should be destroyed. However, transcripts of several of these trials survive. They provide valuable insight into this little known aspect of early nineteenth century life and have therefore been used in writing this chapter.

In late August, Isaac Hitchen, Samuel Stockton, Joseph Holland, Thomas Rix, John Powell, Peter Atherton and Joshua Newman appeared before Sir Robert Graham, charged with sodomy. Two of those arrested in May, Thomas Taylor and John Knight, agreed to turn King's Evidence and they would play leading roles in a number of the trials.

The first of the accused to appear in the dock was wealthy pawnbroker Joseph Holland and the wording of the indictment confirms just how serious the crime he was charged with which he denied, was perceived in early nineteenth century England:

That he not having the fear of God before his eyes, nor regarding the order of nature, but being moved and seduced by the instigation of the Devil on the 9th of July, in the forty-second year of the reign of his present Majesty, at Warrington, in the county of Lancaster, in and upon one Thomas Taylor of

Warrington aforesaid, did make an assault, and that he then and there feloniously, wickedly, diabolically and against the order of nature, carnally knew him, the said Thomas Taylor and did commit the horrid, detestable and abominable crime called buggery.

Taylor described the alleged incident which formed the basis of the charge and which was said to have occurred four years earlier. The witness was a confectioner and was locking up his shop when he was approached by the accused, who invited him to his home for a drink. The witness accepted the invitation, and with Mrs Holland not being at home, he stated that within a few minutes he had agreed to accompany Holland to his bedroom, and the following account was given by Taylor when questioned by the prosecutor.

Q: In what way did you lie down?
A: I lay down on my back.
Q: Did he lie down too?
A: Yes, at my side.
Q: Now state what took place further.
A: He put his private parts between my thighs.
Q: Well?
A: He then asked me to turn on my side, which I did with my bottom towards him. After this he took and put his penis into my fundament [anus].

[The judge intervened and asked the witness for precise details of what happened next]

A: I found myself wet.
Q: What took place when this affair was over?
A: I dressed myself, took up my hat, bid him good night and went home.

This evidence was damning to their client as it confirmed that Holland had ejaculated, which was demanded by the law to establish sodomy had occurred. His lawyers therefore attempted to discredit Taylor and they insisted that he had performed sodomy on many men in the past, but he denied this accusation. He acknowledged that in May following the mass arrests in Warrington, John Knight had accused him of doing so but he had not been charged. He accepted that he had been a passive partner with a number of men but had never committed the crime himself and he vehemently denied having ever blackmailed any of his past partners, nor had he received payment at any time. Furthermore, he was accused of lying about Holland in order to save himself as the following exchange demonstrates during his cross-examination:

Q: Now Sir, I ask you whether at any time after you
      were apprehended, any promises of pardon were
      made to you, provided you would make disclosures
      of what you know respecting the matters then under
      investigation?

A: I was told that if I spoke the truth it would be no
      worse for me.

Q: I must have an answer to the question I put; were
      you not given to understand that if you would tell all
      you know, and make good your story against the
      prisoner, you should not be prosecuted?

A: Yes, I was told if I spoke the truth, I should not.

Q: Not be prosecuted?

A: Yes.

Q: And you expect to be pardoned don't you, if you
      speak the truth?

A: I do.

Judge: If you tell the truth you expect to save your life?

A: Yes, to save my life.

At the conclusion of the prosecution case, three character witnesses were called to speak on Holland's behalf. These included John White, the son of a well known and respected plumber and glazer in Warrington. He advised the court that he had been encouraged by his father to accompany the accused to London, where they spent three weeks. He told of sharing a bedroom with him and insisted that nothing untoward had occurred.

Nevertheless, despite this testimony and the information provided by the other character witnesses who spoke up for him, Holland was convicted of sodomy and sentence was postponed until all the other trials had been completed.

The other man to turn King's Evidence was John Knight, who was a crucial witness in the trial of Thomas Rix, who had invited him to accompany him to Holland's shop. According to the witness, on arriving he noticed that the several men present referred to each other as 'brother', and gave the impression of being a secret society. He testified that Rix had sodomised him and confirmed that he had ejaculated.

Once more, the defence attempted to discredit the witness by claiming that he was lying, as by incriminating the accused, he had been promised a pardon. However, Rix was also convicted of the crime and his sentence too was delayed until the end of all the proceedings.

Knight also testified against John Powell, whose inn at Sankey had been a meeting place for many of Warrington's homosexuals. He told the court of being present at the inn on the occasion of the burial of the accused's sister. There were a number of mourners there, but most of them had left after three or four hours. Knight said he was by then a little drunk, and when he said he was leaving, Powell offered to walk part of the way with him. He alleged that he was sodomised by the accused in a field just off the main road.

Once again the defence claimed the witness was lying to save his own skin, arguing that if such a crime had indeed been committed, Powell would surely have committed it on his own property, and not risk being discovered in the open. Nevertheless, Powell was convicted by the jury.

Knight was also a Crown witness in the trials of Isaac Hitchen and Samuel Stockton, both of whom were convicted of the crime; however, two other men, Joshua Newsham and Peter Atherton were found not guilty, but would not leave the assizes as free men.

John Scott told the court that a group of travelling actors performed in Warrington, and Joshua Newsham invited him to watch the performance from his private box. Afterwards, the two men returned to the defendant's rooms in the public house owned by his brother, where they spent the night together. According to his testimony the witness soon fell asleep and details of what allegedly occurred next emerged in the following exchange with the Crown's barrister:

Q: State what you next observed.
A: Some time in the night I awoke and found the prisoner had got upon my body, with his yard in my fundament.
Q: How long did he remain so?
A: Perhaps two or three minutes. I said 'Oh dear Joseph, what are you doing?' He bid me lie still and I said he should not hurt me any more. He said he would not, and struggling pretty hard he got off.
Q: Did you perceive anything at that time?
A: I did not.

This implied that ejaculation had not occurred and the witness confirmed this was the case when asked directly by the judge. As a result the judge directed that the defendant should be detained in custody to face trial for the non-capital offence of attempted sodomy. This was also the outcome of the trial of seventy-two-year-old Peter Atherton for the same reason, as

Lancaster Castle. Manchester Central Library

the witness, John Hill, failed to convince the court that ejaculation had taken place.

At the conclusion of all the trials of the Warrington defendants, the five convicted men were brought before the judge for sentencing. He stated that they had been convicted of 'a crime not to be named amongst Christians'. He sentenced them all to death and warned them not to expect to be reprieved.

Stockton, Powell and Holland were hanged outside the walls of Lancaster Gaol on Saturday 13 September 1806, alongside Luke Lockard and Peter Higgins who had been convicted of fraud at Salford; and James Yates who was guilty of the brutal rape of a young woman near Rochdale. On the eve of the executions, news was received that those of Hitchen and Rix had been postponed while petitions on their behalf were considered. However, they were not reprieved and the two men were hanged on Saturday 4 October.

CHAPTER 5

The Luddites
1812

Riots in eighteenth and nineteenth century England tended not to be revolutionary in nature, and were usually prompted by specific local issues, which might be the rising cost of theatre tickets, or the presence of the press gang in a town. The most common type however, was the food riot, although this was rarely a simple angry response to an increase in the cost of an item of food. It usually took place arising from a sense of outrage that a dealer in a staple foodstuff was thought to be making unfairly large profits at a time of scarcity and distress. Such disputes were often resolved when local authorities intervened and negotiated a mutually acceptable price.

These public disturbances were more often than not tolerated by the authorities, who viewed them as the inevitable reaction of the population who had no vote, and the means by which they expressed their views. Occasionally, matters would get out of hand and an example would later be made of some of the rioters, who would perhaps face transportation overseas or the gallows. However, in the early years of the nineteenth century the government was faced with what was regarded as one of the most serious threats the state had faced, and the emergence of the Luddite movement led to an unprecedented and massive crackdown.

For several decades, the handloom weavers had enjoyed high wages, but by the early years of the nineteenth century this situation had changed dramatically. The introduction of power looms meant that unskilled workers could now carry out much of the work more quickly and more cheaply. Skilled weavers now found themselves being put out of work or being forced to accept lower wages. This situation was compounded by rapidly increasing food prices due to the Napoleonic wars, and it was against this backdrop that General Ned Ludd first appeared. The mill owners of Nottinghamshire began to receive threatening letters from Ludd, and it was not long before direct action began to be taken, with mills being broken into and the new machines destroyed.

Within a very short time, Luddism had spread to Derbyshire, Leicestershire and Yorkshire, where many disturbances took place. One of the most violent was on 11 April 1812, at Rawford's Mill in Brighouse, which attacked by a large crowd and an attempt was made to break in and destroy the newly installed cloth-finishing machines. However, the owner had arranged for armed guards to watch over his premises, and in the confrontation that followed, two of the rioters were shot dead. The government was so alarmed by events such as this, that the Frame Breaking Act was introduced, which made the destruction of the new machines a capital offence.

The unrest stemming from the distress of weavers had also spread to Lancashire, and by April 1812 the county was in uproar. Attacks on mills in the county included that on 20 April, when a crowd of several thousand attacked the mill owned by Emanuel Burton in Middleton, in which power looms had recently been installed. As the attack on the mill was in progress, the crowd was joined by a group of 200 men, some of whom were armed with muskets, bayonets and pick-axes. At the head of the group a man was carrying a straw effigy of General Ludd, together with a red flag. Trouble, however, had been anticipated, and the military shot dead three of the crowd. On the following day, the enraged mob burnt down the mill owner's house, but not before several more of the protestors had been killed by the military.

That month, there were food riots in Oldham, Ashton and Rochdale, but one of the most serious was the Shudehill Riot in Manchester, on 18 April, when a large crowd comprised mainly of women assembled to protest at the soaring cost of potatoes at Shudehill market. Dealers were charging fifteen shillings per load of 252lbs, and several of the crowd attempted to take some of the vegetables by force. However, the civil authorities intervened and ordered they should be

Shudehill. Manchester Central Library

sold at eight shillings per load. This eased the tension to some extent, but later the premises of dealer John Holland on Deansgate were forcibly entered, and a large quantity of bread, cheese and potatoes were taken. The unrest in the town continued for several more days and on 20 April the cart of John Ramsden, in which he was carrying food, was attacked and all of his produce was removed by force.

Another serious incident occurred at Westhoughton, near Bolton, after a group of forty weavers met on Dean Moor, on 9 April, and resolved to attack the mill belonging to Thomas Wroe and James Duncroft in the near future and destroy the 180 power looms which had been installed there. At noon on Friday 24 April a crowd began to congregate, and by four o'clock about 100 men had assembled. They broke into the mill, and after destroying the machines they set fire to the building. There had been some armed guards present at the scene but too few to prevent the men from achieving their aims and by the time the military arrived the destruction of the building and machinery

Deansgate. Manchester Central Library

had been completed. Nevertheless, a number of eyewitnesses provided the authorities with the names of alleged participants, and a number of arrests followed.

A Special Commission sat in the final weeks of May at Lancaster to deal specifically with those accused of taking part in the disturbances of the previous months throughout the county. Baron Thompson and Sir Simon Le Blanc were the presiding judges, and the list of defendants demonstrates the widespread nature of the unrest and also the significant role played by women.

Twelve men and women were charged with riot at Middleton, and burning down the house and stables of Emanuel Burton, and threatening similar action against the home of his son, Daniel, from whom large quantities of food and alcohol were stolen. Ann Butterworth, Samuel Howarth, Alice Partington, Millicent Stoddard and Ann Dean were convicted of taking part and each was sentenced to six months' imprisonment.

Ann Hamer was fined one shilling for participating in a riot at Barton-Upon-Irwell, and stealing a quantity of flour from the premises of dealer William Taylor. Thomas Brookes was fortunate enough to be acquitted of riot at Pendlebury. John Hope and Samuel Crossley were sentenced to be transported for seven years for their part in a riot at Worsley, during which a mill was broken into and from which grain and flour were removed.

Twenty men appeared for being concerned in the administration of illegal oaths at Bolton, of whom John Hurst, Christopher Metcalf, James Brierley, Henry Thwaite and Thomas Pickup were convicted and sentenced to be transported for seven years.

However, the judges were not to show such leniency to all of those who appeared before them. Fifty-four-year-old Hannah Smith was convicted of highway robbery at Ardwick where she stole butter from a cart, and another offence of riotous assembly with hundreds of others at Bank Top, where potatoes belonging to James Radcliffe were stolen.

Five men and one woman stood trial for participating in the Shudehill Riot and attacking the property of John Holland. Two were acquitted but fifty-year-old John Howarth, John Lee who was forty-six, and twenty-seven-year-old Thomas Hoyle were convicted and sentenced to death.

Twelve men and two women were tried for destroying the weaving mill, warehouse and loom shop at Westhoughton, of whom four were sentenced to death, James Smith, twenty-six-tear-old Thomas Kerfoot, thirty-four-year-old Job Fletcher, and Abraham Charlson who was said to be sixteen years old.

No mercy was to be shown to the eight condemned, and on Saturday 13 June they stood on the scaffold outside the castle. Multiple executions were not uncommon, but the prospect of witnessing such a large group being hanged simultaneously drew a crowd of many thousands, most of whom were sympathetic to those about to die. The authorities feared a rescue attempt and members of the Berkshire Militia and the Oxford Blues were on duty to prevent any problems and to keep order. Abraham Charlson's family made a last desperate plea to the trial judges for mercy, claiming that he was only

Execution.

The last Dying Speeches and Confessions of the Westhoughton
and Manchester

RIOTERS,

Executed at Lancaster, on Saturday the 13th day of June, 1812.

This morning the above unhappy sufferers were brought out
upon the drop behind the castle, severally pinioned, to suffer the law of
sentence of the law. Three companies of the Berkshire Militia were
under arms, and a party of the Oxford Blues stationed in different
quarters, to keep order during the solemn spectacle.

James Smith, aged 31, Thomas Kerfoot, 26, Job Fletcher, 34,
and Abraham Charlson, a youth only 16, made their first appearance,
for being active and setting fire to the Weaving Mill, Warehouse and
Loom-shop, of Thomas Roe and Thomas Duncough, at Westhoughton.

Next appeared John Haworth, aged 30, John Lee, 46, and Thomas
Hoyle, 27, who were severally convicted of riotously assembling with
many more persons, and with breaking and entering in the day time,
the house of John Holland, in Deansgate, Manchester, and stealing a
large quantity of bread, cheese and potatoes.

Hannah Smith.—This misguided female was in the 54th year of
her age, and was tried and convicted of riotously assembling with many
others at Bank Top, Manchester, and committing a high-way robbery
by stealing a quantity of potatoes.

There conduct throughout confinement, manifested the greatest in-
difference and unconcern, as to the awful state in which they were placed: and all the pathetic exhortations of the Reverend the Chaplain,
were frequently repeated before any signs of repentance of their crimes,
or necessity of preparation to meet their God, appeared in any wise to
awaken their benighted minds. Before turned off, however they became penitent, confessed their offences, and with broken and contrite
spirits, cried out to Heaven's Throne to have mercy upon them for miserable sinners.

When we estimate the miserable and deplorability the relatives,
and friends of the unfortunate sufferers feel, must bring from the most
hardened heart, a tear of pity! leaving children without parents, wives
without husbands, and worst of all, the country which gave birth to
their human frame, disobeyed, by not observing before too late,

Short is the day in which ill acts prevail,
But honesty's a rock will never fail.

Plant, printer, Manchester

A broadside giving details of the executions of the Luddites. Author's Collection

thirteen, but there was no reprieve and Abraham died crying out for his mother.

The draconian response of the authorities contributed to the Luddite movement fading away within the next five years, and it proved impossible to prevent the inevitable introduction of powered machinery, which in the years to come would contribute so much to the transformation of the country into a great industrial power.

At the time of the Lancaster executions, John Edward Taylor, a local journalist who was later involved in founding the *Manchester Guardian* newspaper, wrote that he believed the events that had taken place at Middleton had been of the most serious type. However, he claimed that agent provocateurs, in the pay of Colonel Fletcher, a Manchester magistrate, had deliberately encouraged the riot at Westhoughton. His investigations revealed that in the crowd that assembled on Dean Moor in early April, there were as many as ten spies present. The outrage, according to Taylor, could have been prevented, but the authorities allowed it to happen, perhaps not expecting so much damage to be caused, so that an example could be made of those responsible.

The Pendleton Murders
1817

Thomas Littlewood was a wealthy grocer, who lived in the village of Pendleton, two miles distant from his shop in the centre of Manchester. His large and imposing house was set back from the Manchester to Lancaster road and to gain entry to its grounds it was necessary to pass through a large iron gate. Within the fence, a gravel path, which passed the kitchen window, led into a yard where a water pump stood. Close by, was the house of Mr Watkins, a small chapel and cemetery. The area was surrounded by farmland, including Three-nooks Field, and nearby on the main road, were two inns, *The Black Horse* and *The Horse and Shoe.*

Thomas lived in the house with his wife and their two live-in servants, Martha Marsden and the beautiful nineteen-year-old Hannah Partington. Martha had been with the

The Littlewoods' house, where the murders were committed. Author's collection

Littlewoods for ten years and Hannah had worked in the household for two years.

On the morning of Saturday 26 April 1817, Mr and Mrs Littlewood followed their usual custom and left their home to visit the shop, leaving Martha and Hannah on their own in the house. Thomas had left a considerable amount of money in his bedroom drawer, which comprised £160 in notes, nineteen guineas in gold, half a guinea, and seven shilling pieces.

When the Littlewoods returned home at seven o'clock that evening, they were surprised to find the doors to the house locked and the shutters of the kitchen window closed. Thomas found a ladder and entered through an upstairs window. Upon reaching the kitchen he found a large quantity of blood on the floor and covering much of the furniture. Sitting motionless in a chair by the fireplace was Martha, and lying on the floor was the lifeless body of Hannah. A poker and a cleaver lay close to the bodies, and both were smeared with blood. Mr Ollier, a local surgeon, arrived within a short time but there was nothing he could do for the servants, who were declared dead at the scene.

He performed post-mortems on the two victims the following day. There was a wound to Martha's forehead, in which the surgeon placed his finger to discover a fractured skull, and he found a similar wound to the back of her head, and either of these could have killed her. Ollier believed the poker had been used to inflict these injuries. He also discovered a massive fracture to the back of Hannah's skull, and twelve cuts and bruises to her neck, head and breasts. He thought the cleaver had been used against Hannah, which suggested at least two individuals had been responsible for the crimes.

Robbery had been identified as the motive for the brutal murders, as Thomas had found that all of his cash had been stolen, together with a number of his shirts, a dozen silk handkerchiefs, several pairs of stockings, a silver pint jug, six silver tea spoons and three silver table spoons.

Joseph Nadin, Manchester's Deputy Constable, was put in charge of the investigation and in the hours following the

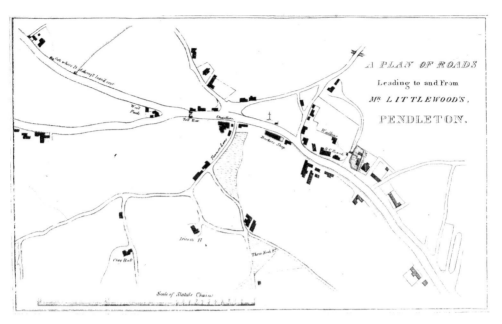

A map of Pendleton. Author's collection

murders, he interviewed a number of witnesses, which led to the names of four local villains emerging as suspects. These were fifty-three-year-old James Ashcroft, his son also named James, who was thirty-two years of age, fifty-three-year-old David Ashcroft, the brother of James senior, and forty-seven-year-old William Holden.

The following morning, Nadin detained David Ashcroft and his nephew James, on St George's Road in Manchester. Nadin took them to James's house first, where a one pound note and five shillings in silver were discovered after a search of the property. At David's house the police discovered a one pound note, and when he was searched seven gold guineas and five one pound notes were found in his pockets. Both were arrested but denied being in Pendleton on the previous day.

On the Sunday evening, James Senior was arrested at his home on Silk Street in Manchester, but nothing was found when the property was searched, and he insisted he had not been involved in the murders. Holden was traced to his lodgings at the *White Hart Inn*, where a search of his room revealed two one pound notes, one guinea, together with nineteen shillings and sixpence in silver. He too insisted that he knew nothing of the crimes in Pendleton. Despite his protestations of innocence and those of the others, the four men were charged with the robbery and murders.

Nadin was confident that he had the right men, for he had several good witnesses to support this view. At 9.30 on the eve of the crimes, William Mortimer, who knew all of the men, saw them in the *Crown and Anchor*. Both he and the landlady spoke to each other of the apparently suspicious manner in which the small group behaved until they left after two hours. There was no laughter or any signs of enjoyment, and they spent the whole of their time in the inn whispering to each other. Nadin was convinced that they were finalising their plans for the robbery and murders they would commit the following day.

Several witnesses were also found who had seen the suspects in the hours immediately preceding the murders. At 11am on the Saturday, John Williams, who was working in a field overlooking the Littlewood home, spoke to young James and David Ashcroft and William Holden, who said they were looking for a house to rent in the village. Later, William Stretch saw the three men close to the Littlewood property, as did Richard Lewis who spoke to young James, who owed him three shillings. At 1pm, James Senior and his son were served in *The Horse and Shoe* by Thomas Chantler. Two hours later, butcher James Burdekin also saw James Senior walking through the village from his shop window. These witnesses clearly undermined the claims of the four men not to have been in the vicinity on the day of the crimes. Furthermore, Nadin found witnesses who enabled him to establish the time the crime took place and that the four suspects were in the area at the time.

James Crompton, a tinker, called at the Littlewood house a little before two o'clock that afternoon, and the door was opened by Martha. Mary Hallows passed the kitchen window as she made her way to the pump a few minutes later. The shutters to the kitchen window were open and inside the room she saw Martha sat in her chair talking to a man not known to the witness, but who she identified later as William Holden. Hannah was in the yard filling a bucket with coal, and she and Mary had a brief conversation.

Hannah Tatterson, who lived nearby, told Nadin that a few minutes after 2pm, she had noticed that the shutters to the kitchen window were closed. Nadin was convinced that the two women were murdered at this time.

At 3pm, Samuel Birtles was sitting in Three-nooks Field, when he saw young James and another man not known to him, being approached by James senior, who was holding a bundle. An hour later, Eli Dyson, a weaver, was on his way to work at Johnson's Mill. He saw James junior who was carrying a bundle, in the company of three men whose identities he did not know. However, the next day he confirmed that they were the three other men being detained by Nadin.

At 4.30pm, the three Ashcrofts were served with ale by Elizabeth Williams at *The Black Horse*, and a customer, John Dunkerley, who had known them for more than twenty years,

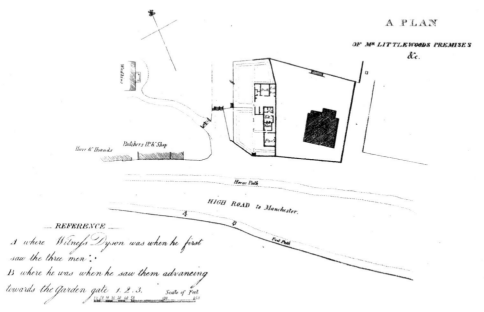

A plan showing the route of witness Eli Dyson as he walked to work. Author's collection

had a conversation with them. These witnesses added further confirmation that these three were in the area on the day of the murders. Another relevant sighting was between 6 and 7 that evening, when Joseph Ramsbottom and Richard Disley were present on a piece of waste ground on Hanover Street in Manchester, where young James and Holden were gambling on a game of pitch and toss. At first, both were betting five shillings a time, but they later challenged their opponents to wager one guinea each toss. From their pockets, each took out several golden guineas and a number of banknotes. Joseph thought this strange as he knew that young James, who was a weaver, had been short of money recently as wages had been very low in the trade during the previous twelve months.

The trial of the four suspects took place at Lancaster on Friday 5 September 1817 before Sir Richard Richards. A fifth man named Simpson had also been arrested and was brought into the dock, but the Crown offered no evidence against him and he was released before the proceedings began. The Crown produced the witnesses found by Deputy Constable Nadin, who could place the prisoners close to the scene of the murders in Pendleton and saw them acting suspiciously on the day they occurred.

Another prosecution witness named William Collins was called, who had been wrongly confined in the New Bailey, on suspicion of stealing a cart. He had shared a cell with James senior, who he described as being disconsolate for much of the time they were together, as he told William he believed he would hang. He later confessed that he had acted as look-out, as the others entered the house and committed the crimes. He was hiding in a field but could be seen from the house, and he was to place his hat on a hedge if anyone approached the building; and he was to give a different signal when it was safe to leave the house.

As the defence case was being opened, the judge asked the accused if they wished to say anything. James senior said: 'It was as impossible for me to do it as pull the sun from the firmament. I never saw the women in my life to my knowledge.' His son followed by saying: 'I never saw the women until I saw them dead. I could not tell if Mrs Marsden was a man or woman. I kissed the innocent lips of Hannah Partington and said I would meet her in heaven with a clear conscience. And so I will my Lord, blessed be to God.'

David Ashcroft insisted that he was '… as innocent as the child unborn, and never heard of it until I was taken up'. William Holden was the last to speak, saying: 'I am as innocent as the child unborn.'

The first defence witness was Adam Haliwell, whose evidence would hopefully discredit that given by William Collins. Haliwell testified that shortly after his release from the New Bailey, Collins had told him that he had indeed discussed the case with James senior, but his cell mate had not confessed, but had in fact claimed that he and the others were innocent.

Robert Deakin testified that he saw James junior at the *White Hart Hotel* on Tassel Street on the Thursday before the crime. He had a large bundle of banknotes and several golden guineas, which he was using to gamble with. This, according to the defence, proved that the money he was found with on the Saturday night was not the proceeds of the crime.

Margaret Mellor swore that she had seen the three Ashcrofts in Manchester at a few minutes to four on the day of the murders, and Margaret Worthington also told of seeing William Holden in another part of Manchester at about the same time. It was claimed that the evidence provided by both of these witnesses demonstrated that none of the accused could have been in Pendleton at the relevant time.

The jury was not persuaded by the defence witnesses and, after retiring for only a few minutes, the four accused were found guilty. They shouted from the dock that they were innocent, and persisted in doing so as the death sentence was passed on each of them. It was then ordered that their executions should take place on the following Monday, outside Lancaster Castle.

On that day, at a little after noon, before a crowd of several thousand, William Holden, already pinioned at the wrists and elbows, was the first to be led on to the scaffold. As the cap was being pulled over his head, he proclaimed his innocence. David Ashcroft was the next to appear and he too shouted that he was innocent. James senior and his son were able to kiss before they too had caps pulled down over their faces. The four men were joined in prayer as they fell through the drop.

Claims that the four men were innocent persisted for many years. On 18 February 1843, an intriguing article appeared in the *Manchester Courier*. It told of the recent death of sixty-year-old John Holden, who was said to have been the uncle of William, who had been living in a notorious district called Egypt. He was reported to have made a deathbed confession to two women in which he admitted to the murders of 1817, and to have declared that his nephew and the Ashcrofts were innocent. One week later, however, the newspaper published the following letter from the Constable of Chowbent:

I wish to inform your readers that the statement is incorrect. I have made every enquiry in connection with the subject, and the two women referred to positively deny that any such statement was ever made. Besides, the man's name was Thomas and not John as stated; he was brother and not uncle to the William Holden who was executed; he was not sixty years of age, and it is stated he was seventy-four; it is also stated he died in Egypt, the fact is he resided at Egypt which is on the Leigh and Westhoughton road, until a few weeks previous to his death, when he removed to a place called Howbridge in the said township, which is Chowbent-within-Atherton, where he died on the 9th instant. Requesting you will have the goodness to insert this letter, will oblige, yours,

John Pemberton, Chowbent, February 23rd 1843.

CHAPTER 7

The Leveson Street Outrage
1849

The increase in crime rates during the early years of the nineteenth century meant that Lancaster was no longer able to cope with the administration of justice in the county. This led to Liverpool becoming an assize town in 1835, after which capital cases could be tried there and executions carried out outside the walls of the Kirkdale House of Correction. The first hanging took place on 24 August 1835. Another ten died on the scaffold there before Maurice Gleeson was executed for committing one of Liverpool's most notorious crimes.

Captain John Hinrickson, his wife Ann and their two sons, five-year-old Henry and three-year-old John, lived at 20 Leveson Street, Liverpool, together with their servant, Mary Parr. It was a large house, situated in a quiet and respectable area. In early 1849, Captain Hinrickson was at sea aboard his ship the *Duncan,* on the return leg of a voyage that had taken him to Calcutta. The Hinricksons were comfortably off but Ann, who was several months pregnant, decided that she would let one of her spare rooms to a lodger, and in March placed a notice to this effect in her front window.

It was four o'clock on the afternoon of Tuesday 27 March that Ann answered a knock at her front door to be met by a seemingly well mannered and respectable looking young man, who told her he was interested in taking the room. He introduced himself as John Wilson, a carpenter at the docks, earning £2 10 shillings weekly. He was invited in and subsequently agreed to take the back parlour and front bedroom.

However, unbeknown to Ann, the caller's real name was Maurice Gleeson, a twenty-seven-year-old Irishman, originally from Brurie, near Limerick. Following the death of his mother he, his three brothers and two sisters had been raised by their father, a blacksmith. However, their father was known in the village as a lazy drunkard who had little positive influence on his children. One of his daughters was transported to Australia for ten years and, facing a robbery charge, Maurice fled and travelled to England. Initially, he lived in Plymouth and London before moving to Liverpool. At the time he called on Mrs Hinrickson he was already living in lodgings on Porter Street.

Within a short time of settling in Liverpool he met and married a young widow, at Christmas in 1846. He had told her that he was an engineer, but it soon became apparent that he had been lying and that he had always worked as a labourer. Furthermore, he was often violent towards her, and with her father's encouragement, she left him. She returned to live with her father in Tranmere, and these events occurred one month before he knocked on the door at 20 Leveson Street.

On the morning of Wednesday 28 March, the lodger left the house at a little after nine o'clock. He encountered Edward McDermott in the street and offered him threepence to call on Mrs Hinrickson, saying he had a letter for John Wilson. This he did, and it would emerge later that this letter stated that the new lodger was not required at work that day.

That afternoon, a delivery boy called at the house and when there was no response to his knocking he looked through the letter box. There, in the entrance hall, he saw a woman lying on the floor and covered with blood. He looked through a front window and saw a child and a young woman, both of whom had been badly beaten. The police arrived at the house within minutes of being contacted and on forcing entry the officers were met by a scene of utter carnage.

It was Ann who was lying in the hallway, still wearing her bonnet and gloves, which like the rest of her, were saturated in blood. Next to her lay a poker, matted with her hair and blood. In the front room they found Mary and Henry, both of whom had suffered massive head wounds. Close to them were a bloodstained shovel and a pair of broken tongs. John's body was discovered in the pantry, and he had suffered a throat wound and a knife was found next to him.

Doctors Martin and Slater arrived at the scene and found that Ann, Mary and Henry had suffered fractured skulls and that the little boy's finger had been cut off. They were still breathing and were taken to Southern Hospital, where mother and son died soon afterwards. Mary would survive them but only for ten days before she too died. John had died instantly for his throat had been cut from ear to ear, his windpipe and carotid artery both having been severed and his head was barely attached to his body.

Despite her injuries Mary Parr was able to make a statement and confirm that their attacker had been the new lodger and to give a very good description, which meant that his details were being circulated throughout the district within a relatively short time of the crime being committed. He had left Liverpool and travelled to Tranmere, where he contacted his estranged wife. He was contrite and, despite his violence towards her in the past, she managed to smuggle him into her bedroom without her father's knowledge.

He remained with her for the night and left early the next morning, after which he spent several hours travelling to and fro on the Birkenhead ferry in an attempt to avoid being recognised on shore and being arrested. However, the captain made him disembark, and the fugitive made his way to the premises of Miert Samuel, a pawnbroker, to whom he offered a gold watch for £30. It was agreed that the two would meet later that day as Miert wished to consult his father before parting with such a large amount of money. When they met again, Miert offered £6, which was agreed to. However, the Samuels had become suspicious and believed he could be the man wanted for the Leveson Street murders. They tricked him into thinking that they had to go to another of their shops some distance away to get the cash.

Miert and Gleeson started to walk to the shop but the route took them past a police station, and as they did so, the public spirited pawnbroker grabbed the suspect and dragged him inside. Superintendent Clough searched him and found a purse and ten shillings and a few pence. The watch was shown to Mrs Harrison, the dead woman's mother who was able to confirm it belonged to her son-in-law, and Mary Nott, a servant girl who worked for the Hinricksons at Leveson Street identified the purse as having belonged to her mistress.

Several witnesses had been traced who could link the suspect to the crime. Edward McDermott identified him as the man who had handed him threepence to deliver the note to Mrs Hinrickson; Michael Kane had seen him wade into a local pond known as the Figure of Eight Pit, close to the murder scene, in which he was washing blood off himself and his clothes. Later, he had purchased a new pair of trousers and changed into them in the shop. Outside, he met Henry Worthington, who told police that he had offered him the old trousers, which Henry later found to be bloodstained. Jane Wilson, a washerwoman on Porter Street, identified him as the man who had sent her a bloodstained shirt to be cleaned. However, perhaps the most damning evidence against him was contained in the deposition taken from Mary Parr on 5 April shortly before she died. The suspect had been present and she was able to identify him as the man who had been responsible for the crime.

Gleeson's trial took place on Wednesday 25 August, before Mr Justice Patterson and given the widespread interest in the case an estimated crowd of 3,000 gathered in the streets surrounding the court building, many of whom attempted to gain entry to the court room.

In line with custom at the time, he was charged with just one murder, that of Mary Parr and the Crown argued that robbery had been the motive. Confronted with overwhelming evidence, the defence argued that Gleeson was insane, but this was rejected by the jury which convicted him at the end of the evidence being given, without leaving their seats.

He was sentenced to death, news of which spread quickly and in the streets could be heard cries of 'He is condemned'. Gleeson could hear the rejoicing crowd as he was escorted by an underground corridor from the court to the Bridewell and told his guards: 'Damn them, I wish I was amongst them.'

Captain Hinrickson had learnt of the murders of his family on arriving at St Helena as he sailed home, and he became more and more depressed as he approached Liverpool. On his arrival he was met by a group of friends who took him to his

Kirkdale Gaol. Author's collection

mother-in-law's home where he would stay for a few weeks. Gleeson had not yet been executed and he expressed a wish to meet the condemned man but was persuaded to abandon this plan. After settling his affairs in Liverpool he travelled to Hull to stay with relatives.

Gleeson was to be hanged at noon on Saturday 15 September and by six o'clock on the Friday evening, several hundred people had gathered outside Kirkdale Gaol to claim a good vantage point. The notoriety of his crimes meant that special trains were laid on from towns throughout the North West, and it was estimated that more than 100,000 spectators witnessed Gleeson being put to death.

In December 1850, the town council decided to change the name of Leveson Street to its original name of Grenville Street South. This followed complaints from local residents that property values in the street had fallen greatly since the murders.

CHAPTER 8

The Case of the Spanish Sailor
1863

Throughout the first half of the nineteenth century the number of capital crimes gradually decreased and the last individual to be executed for attempted murder was hanged in 1861, after which only those convicted of murder would stand on a gallows in Lancashire.

At a few minutes after nine on the night of Tuesday 12 May 1863, James Harrison, Henry Cohen and John Howells left Mr Mott's public house on Oldhall Street, each man having drunk tuppence worth of whisky. They were merry but by no means drunk as they walked towards Fazackerley Street. On reaching the corner of the street Henry bumped accidentally into a young man, who immediately pulled a knife from his jacket and stabbed him before running away.

Henry fell to the ground and John remained with him while James ran in pursuit of the attacker. A few moments later, John looked on in horror as the man also stabbed his other friend, who had caught up with him, before disappearing into the darkness.

Both of the wounded men were taken to the Northern Hospital where they were treated by Dr Newton Heelis. Henry had suffered a wound to his back and at first it was thought this would be fatal, but he would survive. James was found to have suffered a deep wound to his stomach, exposing his bowels, and he died twenty minutes after his arrival. A post-mortem revealed that the fatal wound had cut into his liver and the cause of death was haemorrhaging and shock.

Meanwhile, the police detained a Spanish seaman, named Miguel Barno, as he fitted the description of the knifeman. He was taken to the hospital, but at an identity parade at the side of Henry's bed, the injured man failed to identify him and he was thus released.

However, it was not long before the police received information from Antonio Bargos who kept a lodging house for foreign sailors visiting Liverpool. He reported that at 9.30, on the night the attacks occurred, one of his lodgers, Jose Alvarez, a cook on the brigantine *Pepita* currently berthed in Victoria Dock, had been acting suspiciously. He arrived at the lodgings in a breathless state as though he had been running. When asked by his landlord the reason, Alvarez had replied: 'I have come from Oldhall Street and I have been fighting with two or three Englishmen.' He continued by saying one of them had pushed him and they had poked fun at him. They ignored his pleas to stop taunting him and he had taken out his knife saying to his landlord: 'It is better to be in prison than in the cemetery, because they were three against me.' Having heard this account, Antonio ordered Alvarez to leave his house and approached the police.

Alvarez was soon traced to a brothel on Pennington Street where he was arrested, and he was later identified as the knifeman by several witnesses to the incident, but no knife was found on him.

The Northern Hospital. Liverpool Central Library

The inquest into James Harrison's death was held before the coroner, Mr PF Curry, on 15 May, at which identification of the body was provided by his sister, Mary. One of his companions, John Howells, third mate on the ship *Calloon*, told the coroner's court that they had not been drunk and had not taunted or pushed the accused man. Three youngsters, James Powner, James Shuttleworth and Griffith Jones, testified that they had witnessed Alvarez stab the men, and Elizabeth Bray also told of seeing him stab James Harrison. Hannah Moore told the court that she had seen him with a knife in his hands as he left the scene. The coroner's jury found that Alvarez was guilty of wilful murder, and he was committed to stand trial at the next assizes.

The twenty-two-year-old accused man was a native of Cadiz, where his parents and five sisters lived. When he was seventeen years of age he joined his first ship, and had remained a seaman since then. His trial took place on Monday 17 August before Mr Justice Blackburn, when he was charged with the murder and attempted murder of Henry Cohen who had made a full recovery. Mr Conway and Mr Peel represented the Crown and Alvarez was represented by Mr Russell. The Spanish consul acted as interpreter for the accused man. Evidence was given by those who had testified at the inquest and the trial ended at a few minutes before four o'clock in the afternoon. The jury returned after thirty minutes with a guilty verdict, but they added a strong recommendation for mercy. The judge seemed surprised at this and asked the jury foreman on what grounds the recommendation was made, and was told: 'On account of him being a foreigner and not understanding the English language.'

The judge sought further clarification and said: 'I understand you to mean gentlemen, that although you do not think that sufficient to justify you in saying that it mitigated the offence from murder to manslaughter, yet it is a matter which somewhat palliates the offence?'

The foreman confirmed this was the case, but in sentencing Alvarez to death the judge warned him that he should not expect a reprieve. The judge proved to be correct and Alvarez was hanged outside Kirkdale Gaol on Saturday 12 September 1863.

CHAPTER 9

A Wayward Son
1866

In 1864, Manchester followed Liverpool in becoming an assize town which resulted in capital trials being heard there. A new county gaol to be built at Strangeways had been in the planning process for several years but construction had not yet begun. For a period in the 1860s, the New Bailey, which had been built in Salford towards the close of the eighteenth century, would therefore be the site of the district's executions.

Robert Burrows was the landlord of the *Hopwood Arms* at Slattocks, close to the village of Hopwood, where he lived with his three daughters and eighteen-year-old son, James. He also owned a farm close to the inn, and on Saturday 19 May 1866 Robert hired forty-year-old Irish itinerant farm worker, John Brennan, who was to start work on the following Monday morning. On Sunday evening, John visited another local public house, the *Jolly Waggoner,* where he introduced himself to his new employer's son. James Burrows was sat with a group of friends and at some point, a bet was laid and John lent James half-a-crown, which was paid back later that night.

James returned to the *Jolly Waggoners* at ten o'clock the following morning and drank a few beers with his friend, Henry Clegg. They were joined later by James Taylor, nicknamed 'Germany', who worked as a brewer at the inn. At three in the afternoon, James and Henry left the hostelry having run out of money. James said he wanted to continue drinking in nearby Rochdale. He decided he would go and see his father's new labourer, as he knew from the previous evening that he had plenty of cash because he had loaned him half-a-crown. The two friends walked to a field, which John had just finished ploughing and Henry watched James approach John who was unyoking the horse. The two men entered the farm building which acted as the stables and cowshed, and fifteen minutes later James emerged alone. Henry asked: 'How hast thou gone on?' to which James replied: 'He would not lend me a damned halfpenny', and the pair returned to the *Jolly Waggoner.*

Meanwhile, a boy found the horse he knew belonged to Mr Burrows, wandering along a lane unattended. He returned the horse to the stables and fastened the door without entering the building. Later, Isabella, the sister of James, went to the stables to feed the horse and discovered the body of John Brennan. He was lying on his back on the ground having suffered serious head injuries. She presumed he had been kicked by the horse and raised the alarm.

When James and Henry had first entered the inn, Alice Chatburn the landlady noticed that before ordering a drink, James made for the washroom before approaching Germany with whom he spoke briefly. They next left the premises, and she watched as they began to fight each other. James failed to land a punch, but his opponent bloodied his nose, after which the two men returned to the bar. Alice thought it strange that the two men still appeared to be on good terms. After a few minutes Isabella rushed into the bar to advise her brother of finding the body. James left with her, but returned ninety minutes later at six o'clock, and had several more drinks before leaving one hour later saying he had to milk his father's cows.

That night, James did not sleep in his own bed. Instead, he slept in a haystack, accompanied by Germany, in one of his father's fields, which was opposite the *Jolly Waggoner.* At five o'clock the next morning, the two men were wakened by a loud noise, and saw two policemen banging on the door of the inn. James hurried away, telling his friend that he had to start work on the farm. When he arrived home, Isabella told him that the police wished to interview him, and he promised to go and see them later that morning.

Rochdale surgeon Frederick Booth performed a post-mortem on the afternoon of Wednesday 23 May. He found injuries to both eyes, and deep head wounds, all of which exposed the skull, a portion of which had been driven into the brain. Death had been caused by damage to the brain caused by the fractures. The surgeon was adamant that the injuries were not consistent with the deceased having been kicked by a horse, and that some kind of blunt instrument had been used, meaning that this had not been an accidental death but he had been murdered.

Sergeant Simpson and Constable Hicks searched the stables and when a part of the wall was removed, they discovered a small cavity in which they found a crowbar bearing traces of blood and of human hair similar to that of the dead man. Later on the Tuesday morning the officers interviewed Germany who realised from the manner in which he was questioned that he was a suspect. He therefore decided to co-operate fully, and told them that James had shown him the crowbar on the previous evening.

Germany also gave details of the sham fight he had with his friend on the previous afternoon. He explained that Burrows had approached him in the washroom of the inn, where he was working. There was blood on his collar and necktie, which James removed and threw into the boiler to burn them. As he washed himself, he told Germany: 'I have killed yon bugger in the stable', and continued by describing how he had inflicted the fatal injuries with the crowbar, which he later showed him. It was then that Burrows proposed they should pretend to argue and fight, so he would be able to explain how he came by any bloodstains that might be found on him.

James had not reported to the police as he promised his sister he would, and a search for him was begun. Late Tuesday afternoon, Sergeant Simpson found him hiding amongst the hay in his father's barn. There were bloodstains on his trousers, which he claimed must have got there when he had earlier helped move the body, and when charged with the murder he replied: 'I did not do it.'

Burrows stood trial at the August Manchester Assizes, and pleaded not guilty. The most damning testimony against him was that provided by Germany who claimed that the accused man had confessed to the crime a matter of minutes after committing it. The defence case was based on the proposition that Germany was the real culprit, and to support this claim

New Bailey Gaol. Manchester Central Library

details of his previous bad character were given to the jury. When serving in the Army he had been imprisoned for desertion; he had been tried for dishonesty matters at the Liverpool Assizes and Salford Sessions; and he had served a prison term for vagrancy. The defence lawyers argued that even if the jury did not believe the witness to be the murderer, they should not send their client to the gallows solely on the evidence of such a dishonest and untrustworthy man.

An example of the accused's past bravery was given to the jury, to highlight the more positive aspects of his character. Twelve months earlier, a farmer and his son were returning home with a cow, and the youngster had the halter around his waist. They encountered a local hunt, and the cow became alarmed by the pack of hounds and bolted in panic, dragging the boy with it. The cow rushed thirty yards before falling into the canal together with the terrified boy who was now in danger of being drowned. James Burrows had immediately leapt into the canal, and at great danger to himself due to the now even more panic-stricken beast, released the boy and carried him to safety. This, it was claimed, was not the behaviour of a callous murderer.

The trial judge gave a very fair summing up at the close of the trial which had lasted ten hours. The jury found Burrows guilty of murder, but there was a strong recommendation for mercy because of his youth. He was sentenced to death and as he awaited his execution, his solicitor, Mr Bent, organised a petition for a reprieve which was well supported in the district. However, the following letter was received:

Sir, I am directed by Mr Secretary Walpole to acknowledge the receipt of your letter Of the 10th instant, forwarding a memorial on behalf of James Burrows, sentenced to death for murder; and I am to acquaint you that after a careful consideration of the facts, Mr Walpole regrets that he has not felt it consistent with his public duty to advise Her Majesty to interfere with the due course of law in this case.

I am sir, your obedient servant,

H WADDINGTON

Mr E Bent, 21 Bridge Street, Manchester

The execution of Burrows, which was to take place at 8am on Saturday 25 August 1866, would be the first in the Manchester and Salford area since that of croft-breaker George Russell who was hanged at Newton Heath in 1798. The prison and local authorities were determined that there should be no mishaps, and began the preparations on the preceding Thursday, when part of the gaol wall on New Bailey Street was demolished, so that work could begin on erecting the scaffold.

When the gaol had been designed and built towards the close of the eighteenth century, it had not been envisaged that it would become the site for public executions. There were thus real concerns that some form of catastrophe could occur in the narrow streets surrounding the gaol, and also given its proximity to the River Irwell in which it was feared many could drown if the crowd was not properly controlled. A large number of crash barriers were therefore erected to hopefully ease the pressure of the many thousands of spectators who were expected to attend the event.

Thomas Wright, Manchester's prison philanthropist. National Portrait Gallery

Crowds began to gather in the vicinity from 3am, and many of these were women, who were not deterred by hoax notices that had been put up reading:

> Borough of Salford: All females attending the execution will be taken into custody and detained till two o'clock the same day – By Order

By 7.30am, an estimated crowd of 50,000 had arrived, and these included the usual pickpockets, hoping for rich pickings, and street preachers exhorting those present to take warning from what they were about to witness. Shopkeepers and householders made a great deal of money by renting out their rooms which overlooked the scene.

At 7.55am, Burrows appeared on the scaffold, accompanied by Manchester's well-known prison philanthropist, Thomas Wright. Five minutes later, Burrows had died without incident at the hands of hangman William Calcraft.

CHAPTER 10

Lancashire's Last Public Hangings
1867

By late 1867, Mary Hamner, a twenty-six-year-old single Irish woman, who worked in a local cotton mill, had been a lodger of Mary Broderick in Moorgate Street, Droylsden, for seven years. Timothy Faherty, a thirty-six-year-old cotton operative, had also lodged in Mrs Broderick's house for four months, but had left in mid October that year. During his stay at Moorgate Street he had grown fond of young Mary, and had admitted this to his landlady. However, Mary had made it clear that she did not have similar feelings for Faherty, as she considered him to be a drunkard. Nevertheless, after he left the lodgings Faherty continued to visit the house to see Mary and was on reasonably good terms with her.

When Faherty visited Mary during the afternoon of Christmas Day 1867, there were no indications of the tragic and bloody events that would soon occur. He told her of his plans to visit Ireland, and Mrs Broderick's daughter, Bridget, who was with them, heard Mary tell him: 'Give my respects to the green fields and the shamrock.' The couple seemed to be on good terms, when Bridget left them to go to her bedroom for a nap.

From her bed, Bridget heard Mary walk into the kitchen and Faherty follow her a few moments later. She next heard Mary shouting: 'Get off with you, why have you come in here after me?' Bridget heard nothing more and eventually drifted off to sleep, but was awakened when Mary burst through her bedroom door, her face covered with blood, screaming: 'Bridget, I am killed!' Faherty followed a few steps behind her, carrying a poker, with which he struck Mary on the head. Mary fell to the floor onto her knees, and Bridget watched helplessly as Faherty closed the door behind him. He struck

Mary across the head once again, shouting: 'I'll kill you!' repeatedly.

Faherty dropped the poker and Bridget took advantage to run from the room, despite his attempt to prevent her from doing so by grabbing her hair. Downstairs, she found several neighbours, who had been alerted by the screams and had rushed to the house. Thomas Brown and Mary Alundale went upstairs where they discovered Mary lying apparently lifeless on the floor, with Faherty kneeling over her, who cried out: 'I've killed her. I gave her my honour and I love her and I am here to die for her.'

Thomas told Faherty to raise her into a sitting position and attempted to encourage her to take a drink of water. However, she could not swallow, and could only make gurgling sounds. Dr Robert Slater was called for and arrived within minutes, but he could not save Mary who died shortly after he arrived. Dr Slater performed a post-mortem and discovered a number of serious facial and head injuries. There were four extensive wounds to the back of her head, two of which had resulted in skull fractures, which he concluded had been the cause of death.

Faherty's sudden uncontrollable violent outburst appeared to have been due to his anger at yet another rejection by Mary of his advances. At his trial the following March, it was argued that he had not visited the lodging house with the intention of killing her, for he took no weapon, and when Bridget went to bed, the couple were on good terms. This it was argued by the defence, suggested there was an absence of malice aforethought, and he should be convicted of manslaughter. However, it did not take the jury long to find Faherty guilty of murder, after which he was sentenced to death.

There was a second murder trial at the March Assizes that had created a nationwide sensation, and that was of twenty-three-year-old Todmorden weaver, Miles Wetherhill, who was accused of murdering Jane Smith.

It was some minutes after ten o'clock on the night of Monday 2 March 1868, and Reverend Anthony Plow of Christ Church, Todmorden had just arrived home at the vicarage following a visit to a parishioner. He was about to retire to bed,

Christ Church and Vicarage. Todmorden Antiquarian Society

but there was a loud banging on the back door, and suspecting it was Miles Wetherhill, with whom he had been experiencing some difficulties in the preceding weeks, he advised his three servants, Jane Smith, Elizabeth Spinks and Mary Hodgson, to keep away from the back door. Reverend Plow went out by the front door, and on reaching the back of the building he saw Wetherhill who was holding an axe; and who upon seeing Reverend Plow immediately lunged at him, badly injuring the vicar's hand. Wetherhill next pulled a pistol from his coat, and taking aim, pulled the trigger. However, the gun did not fire and, using the axe, he struck the vicar on the head. Unlocking the door, Wetherhill dragged the almost unconscious vicar into the vicarage, continuing to strike him across the head as he did so.

The three servants rushed to their master's aid, grabbing his attacker by the hair, which enabled the vicar, who was losing a large amount of blood, to escape through the front door. Elizabeth Spinks ran to find help as the other two young women continued to struggle with Wetherhill. He began screaming at Jane Smith, saying that she was a liar and had been 'telling tales' about him. He managed to struggle free and lock the back door. He turned and struck Jane with the axe so severely that her hand was almost severed. She fled into the dining room, screaming in terror and pain. She slammed the door but he forced his way in and with another pistol he had brought with him, shot her.

The vicar's wife was resting in bed with her new-born baby daughter, Hilda, and was being attended to by her nurse, Margaret Ball. The nurse heard the disturbance and left the bedroom to investigate. Looking downstairs, she saw Wetherhill loading the pistol and then picking up the poker. He extinguished the gas lights and walked up the stairs. At the top, he approached the bedroom in which Mrs Plow was resting, but Margaret attempted to block his way, saying: 'Those you want are downstairs.' He replied: 'I have finished them, but you needn't be afraid for you've done me no harm.'

He pushed her aside and entered the bedroom. He pulled back the sheets and fired the pistol at Mrs Plow, but

Reverend Plow. Todmorden Antiquarian Society

Mrs Plow. Todmorden Antiquarian Society

fortunately missed. He began to beat her with the poker, but by now two neighbours had entered the house. They were Mr Gledhill, the parish clerk, and Mr Spinks, who grabbed Wetherhill before he could inflict serious injuries.

Wetherhill was a local man, who had been raised by his widowed mother and grandparents. He was a weaver by trade, and had been active in the church for many years. This was how he met sixteen-year-old Sarah Bell, who had arrived at the vicarage as a thirteen-year-old nursemaid but who later became a cook, and who Wetherhill had been courting for several months.

After they had been seeing each other for several weeks, Wetherhill had arranged to meet Reverend Plow to advise him of the relationship and his intentions towards her. The vicar expressed his initial opposition, having assured Sarah's parents that he and Mrs Plow would be responsible for her welfare. Nevertheless, as he knew the young man well, he promised to discuss it with Mrs Plow. The outcome of this discussion was that Wetherhill was warned that he must stop seeing Sarah, and he was barred from visiting the vicarage under any circumstances. Furthermore, Sarah was not allowed to leave the vicarage on a Sunday, which was her only day off.

Despite these obstacles, the young couple continued to meet in secret, but when the Plows became aware of this, Sarah was dismissed for what they considered to be a serious breach of trust. On 30 October 1867, Sarah sent a letter to Wetherhill advising him she was returning home to Yorkshire and she wrote:

Dear Miles,
Please do not come anymore because there has been such a row. My dear Miles I am sorry to disappoint you, but mother says it cannot be now, for one thing – you must guess the rest as I have to do, but I can tell you it is quite as great

Sarah Bell. Todmorden Antiquarian Society

a disappointment to me as it is to you. If it is convenient for you to be at the station on Friday at seven o'clock, I should so much like to see you again. It is hard to part with you my own dear boy, but you must not fret. You know it is 'hard-hearted, long-parted', so I must say good night my dear for it is bed time. I remain yours ever,

Sarah

So it was that on 1 November they met at the station, and Wetherhill decided to travel to Yorkshire with her. They spent two days together, before he returned to Todmorden, and it was soon after this that Sarah found a position at The Friend's Retreat in York. They kept in contact by letter, and Wetherhill continued to attempt to persuade Sarah to return to Todmorden, and writes of his anger with the Plows, and also with Jane Smith, as he blamed her for telling her employers of his assignations with Sarah.

Miles Wetherhill. Todmorden Antiquarian Society

In a letter to Sarah, dated 7 November, he expresses his continuing love for her, and describes his sense of resentment, and his sense of betrayal by individuals he does not name:

> My Dear Sarah, I am now at Todmorden once more. You know how we love each other, and you may guess how I have been since. Oh Sarah, My true love, how I do long to see you. I should so like to view that sweet face of yours once more. I hearkened many hours in the yard at the kitchen door, but them times is gone – gone. I am sorry to say for ever. I wish I had staid a bit longer, as you wanted me for I only worked four hours. I wish you were at Todmorden again. I should then be happy once more, but now I am miserable. We are parted, and what is it for? Not for any disgraceful action either of us has done. No, it is for being too honourable and upright in our dealings. Sarah, it makes my blood boil to think of the wrong they have done to you. I will never forgive them. They have ruined our happiness.

Another letter, dated 11 November, gives details of a confrontation with the Plows:

> My Dear Sarah Elizabeth, you must excuse me for writing so much but this will be the last time for a bit. I have had such a row with master and mistress. I had heard she had given you a character so I asked her about it, and she put it in what you told me she would. It was yesterday noon when I saw her, and she said she thought there was not much wrong in it, but I told her there was a great deal of wrong in it. In the afternoon I saw the master. He called on me and we had a regular row. He called us anything but Christians and spoke of you not being a respectable girl. He made my blood boil and I will have my revenge for the girl I love unless you can come to Todmorden, or within a mile or two of it, so that we may plague them by walking out.

On 19 November, he wrote asking her to return to Todmorden, criticizes the Plows, and he also mentions Jane Smith for the first time:

Ah Sarah, how happy we should be if you could get a place here, and then we could have our walk and plague them. They are, I understand, going to have a cook on Tuesday. She is coming from where Jane the traitor comes from. But now we are not together and if you love me you will come. Oh Sarah, come and don't let us be parted, for it is hard to be parted from the one I love. If you were poorly it would be a different thing, but you are well and healthy, and so let us enjoy our youth in spite of the Plows. Why can't you get a place without being so far away? Letter courting is not like courting personally, and we should not have had any cause to be parted at all if it had not been for the Plows, Plow and his wife have spoilt our happiness and unless that happiness can be renewed they shall rue it. I cannot forgive them for doing as they have done towards us.

Jane Smith. Todmorden Antiquarian Society

Wetherhill spent the weekend before the crime with Sarah in York. Once again he pleaded with her to return to Todmorden, but she told him she was happy in her new position and intended staying there. A despondent Wetherhill left York on the Monday and on reaching Todmorden met an old friend, Samuel Lord, with whom he spoke for some time. Samuel asked him why he did not simply marry Sarah and bring her to Todmorden as his bride. Wetherhill replied by saying: 'It takes two to get married.' Clearly, he must have begun to realise Sarah would never return, and that the relationship was possibly at an end.

Later, he met a group of friends for a drink, but he left them in the public house at a little before ten o'clock. He told them he was going home, but instead called at the *Black Swan*, where he had a whisky, before walking towards the vicarage. What none of his friends had realised was that he had decided to take his revenge on those he blamed for his unhappiness. Earlier that night he had visited the shop of ironmonger John Hollinsworth, and asked that his flask be filled with the best gunpowder. He also bought a number of caps and four ounces of shot. Furthermore, he had armed himself with the axe and four pistols, which were held in his belt, into which he had cut four slits to hold them.

To the police, who arrested him at the scene of his crime, this was evidence that he had not acted in a spontaneous passionate rage, but that he had given the matter a great deal of thought, and he had selected his intended victims with care. For instance, he could simply have attacked all of the servants, especially Margaret Ball, who had attempted to bar his way into Mrs Plow's bedroom, but he had not done so. Once in the bedroom, he had taken one-month-old Hilda from her arms, and placed her gently in her cradle, without harming her, before attacking Mrs Plow.

Jane Smith was buried on 3 March, and despite apparently recovering from his injuries, Reverend Plow died on 12 March. Coincidentally, the Plows' baby daughter Hilda died on the same day, but for reasons not associated with the crime, and Mrs Plow continued to make a good recovery from her physical injuries. The inquest into Reverend Plow's death was held at

Jane's grave. Todmorden Antiquarian Society

the *Black Swan* on the day after he died. Despite it being found that he had died as a result of the injuries inflicted by Wetherhill, the trial was not postponed, and his attacker was not charged with his murder. This meant that when he appeared before Mr Justice Lush, he faced only one murder charge, that of Jane Smith.

The prosecution presented the murder as a callous crime, which had been carefully planned by the accused. The defence however suggested that their client was insane. During the trial, it emerged that Jane Smith had not informed the Plows of Sarah's continuing relationship with Wetherhill, and it seemed that it was Sarah who had inadvertently done so.

In his summing up, the judge emphasised to the jury that although Weatherhill had committed a diabolical crime, this in itself did not mean that he was insane, and no medical evidence had been called by the defence to prove this. The jury did not leave their seats and after conferring for a matter of moments, the foreman announced a guilty verdict.

In sentencing him to death, the judge described the crime as like a murder that had been committed by 'a wild savage rather than a person brought up and nurtured in civilised life'. After the condemned man had been taken from the dock, the judge ordered that the Plows' servants should receive cash awards to mark the bravery each had shown at the time of the murder.

Faherty and Wetherhill were hanged together on Saturday 4 April 1868, outside the New Bailey Gaol. It was recognised that these would probably be the last executions to take place in public in Lancashire, as the Private Executions Act was expected to become effective within a short time. Several hundred had gathered outside the gates of the Salford gaol by midnight, and eight hours later, an estimated 20,000 spectators were eagerly waiting to witness the two young men die. The executions were scheduled for 8am, and the crowd was in a boisterous and almost celebratory mood as the hour approached. A circle was formed and a prize fight organised for entertainment; many pigeon fanciers had travelled from throughout the country, and released the birds, which they had brought with them.

As the two condemned were led out onto the scaffold Faherty could be seen to be trembling violently, but in contrast, Wetherhill, whose wax model was already on show in Madame Tussaud's London showroom, was incredibly calm. The executioner, William Calcraft, who often displayed a callous disregard to the feelings of those he was about to hang, was heard to comment that the Todmorden weaver was the most self-possessed individual he had ever executed.

Wetherhill died instantly, but Faherty struggled for a short time. They were cut down after one hour and buried within the prison walls. They were indeed the last to hang in the county, and just three more public executions occurred nationally in the coming weeks, with the last public hanging taking place outside Newgate Gaol on 26 May.

CHAPTER 11

A Double Hanging
1874

In May 1868, Parliament passed legislation ending public executions. In future, hangings would take place behind prison walls, but prison governors and county sheriffs had the discretionary authority to allow representatives of the press and the relatives of victims to attend.

In February 1874, leaving his wife at home in Glasgow, Henry Flannigan, a twenty-two- year-old shoemaker, travelled south to Liverpool to start a new job as foreman in his aunt's shoe and boot making business, at 7 Bent Street, off Scotland Road. Fifty-three-year-old widow Mary Flannigan had also agreed that her nephew could live on the premises as did three other of her employees, named Ryan, Meehan and Flynn.

All seemed to go well until the night of Saturday 4 April. After the day's work had been completed, the four men bought a large quantity of beer to drink in the house and it was not too long before all of them were drunk. At 8.30pm, Mary's daughter, Ann McMurray, called at the house just as Henry was leaving. They bumped into each other accidentally and as they did so a pair of new boots fell from underneath his jacket.

Ann accused him of stealing her mother's property, a charge he denied, claiming that Mrs Ryan had given them to him to take next door where Mary's sons James and Daniel also had a shoemaking business. This was denied by Mrs Ryan, and on being informed of what had happened Mary accused her nephew of stealing the boots with the intention of pawning them so that he could buy more alcohol. An argument followed, which led to Daniel and James being informed of what had happened. When they arrived Daniel punched his cousin, who immediately cried out that someone would pay that night.

However, the argument subsided and Mary's sons left the house believing that Henry, who had eventually admitted attempting the steal the boots, would not carry out what seemed to be an empty and drunken threat. Flynn left the house with the brothers to sleep in their house, and Ryan and Meehan went upstairs to their own beds leaving Henry and Mary alone in the kitchen. However, nothing was heard by anyone during the night as both appeared to have calmed down and settled their differences. At about 4.30am the next day, Mrs Ryan made her way downstairs to light a fire in one of the rooms. She looked into the kitchen and in the dim light noticed nothing unusual.

Three hours later, Flynn returned to his employer's house and was let in by Mrs Ryan. Henry woke up, and still the worse for drink, went upstairs saying he was going to bed to sleep off his hangover. Nevertheless, within a few minutes he was asking the other men if they wanted to go to a local public house with him. They declined the invitation and went downstairs, where they discovered Mary's body in the kitchen. Henry came downstairs, and was immediately confronted by the others who accused him of being responsible for her death as she had been the victim of a vicious attack. He denied any knowledge of what had happened, but by the time the police arrived Henry had left the house carrying all of his tools having told the others he was going to Manchester to look for work.

The police found Mary lying on her back on the floor with her head resting on a waistcoat which was later found to be Henry's. Her clothing had been disarranged, her skirt having been pulled up above her waist. Surgeon John Cormack confirmed that she had been dead for about three hours and performed a post-mortem the next day. There was bruising to the left side of her throat, and marks on her hands suggesting she he had been dragged along the floor. In his opinion death had resulted from suffocation or strangulation, probably the former. Her killer had possibly covered her face with a pillow. Her heart was healthy and an examination of her stomach contents showed that she had not been drinking alcohol before she met her death. He also revealed that she had been the victim of a brutal rape.

When he left 7 Bent Street, Henry met George Neill, also a shoemaker, who worked next door for Mary's sons. He was unaware of Mary's death and Henry asked him to travel to Manchester to look for work, but George declined. However, he did agree to accompany him to Prescott after Henry promised to treat him to a few drinks.

George would later inform the police that his companion used a number of sovereigns to buy food and drink. When he asked him how he had come by so much cash, Henry replied: 'I'll tell you all about it George. I had a tussle with my aunt. She was drunk and I took a purse from her breast. I took some money from it and put it back again. I thought I would have to do for her, but she was not dead when I left her.' He also said that he had attempted unsuccessfully to rape her.

They arrived in Prescott at noon but parted company as Henry decided to travel to Glasgow. George remained in Prescott overnight and was arrested the following day for being drunk and disorderly. Henry, however, did not get very far for he was arrested on the Sunday night by Constable James Swarbrick, who found him lying on a footpath in Knotty Ash, obviously very drunk. He claimed to have recently arrived in the area from Glasgow and denied any connection with Liverpool. However, he was detained as he fitted the description of the man wanted for the Bent Street murder. When later charged with the murder he replied: 'It can't be helped now.'

When his trial opened at Liverpool's August Assizes he pleaded not guilty. The Crown claimed that in a drunken rage, he had attacked his aunt, and had also ravished her. Having killed her he decided to steal the cash he knew she carried on her person. It was acknowledged that when he awoke on the Sunday morning he might not have recalled what he had done, but when it gradually dawned on him after the body was discovered, he took flight.

In his defence it was argued she had died of apoplexy and thus of natural causes. He had fled the house because he feared for his safety as he believed her sons would attack him. The alleged confession to George Neill was particularly damning and Henry's lawyer attempted to discredit the evidence and to imply he may have been responsible for the crime. He admitted that his real name was Edward Neill and that he had served several prison sentences in his native Ireland and in England. However, the jury was satisfied that Henry was the culprit as he was convicted and sentenced to death.

There was another murder trial at the August Assizes and once again alcohol played a significant part in the crime. On Monday 20 April, there had been a violent disturbance in Raleigh Street, Bootle which involved a number of women who lived in the street, and all of whom were drunk. Among them was thirty-year-old Mary Williams who lived with her husband and seven children, at number 60 in the street. She argued with the two Manning sisters who lived at number 50, and at one point the sisters were seen by Mary Carling to be holding Mary down on the ground by her hair and punching her. Mrs Carling urged them to stop but they threatened to attack her if she did not move on. Eventually, those involved in the disturbance returned to their homes and the street was quiet once more.

However, at nine o'clock that night, Nicholas Manning, the twenty-six-year-old brother of the battling sisters, called at Mary's house. Neighbours heard raised voices as he stepped into the hallway. She was heard to order him to leave and as he stepped outside he shouted: 'I have never struck a woman in my life.' A gunshot was heard almost immediately and he collapsed to the pavement, holding his right side. He was taken to Bootle Hospital for emergency treatment.

Constable Whitworth was the first police officer at the scene and he interviewed a number of neighbours who had witnessed the day's events. Seconds before the shot was fired Mary was heard shouting: 'I'll give you a mark you will carry to the grave.' Another heard her say after the shooting: 'Yes, and there are two or three more I will do it to before the night is over.' He also received information that after the wounded man had been taken to hospital, Mary said: 'If that won't do, I'll shoot him in the back.' Furthermore, James and Jane Wardle reported seeing her produce the gun from underneath her apron and firing it at the injured man.

On the basis of these statements, the constable made a search of Mary's house. He discovered a powder flask, a box of caps, nine bullets and a ramrod under her bed. He found another flask hidden in a clock case, and on examining the fireplace found the loaded gun used in the shooting, hidden in the ashes. On the way to the local police station Mary told the constable: 'It's all right, it is me done it and I would do it again.' Later that night, when charged with attempted murder she responded by saying: 'No not to murder him, I only did it to frighten him.'

A deposition was taken from Nicholas as he lay in his hospital bed three days after the shooting, and he stated that he had a clear view of the arrested woman holding the gun and shooting him. The wounds proved fatal and he died on Sunday 26 April of blood poisoning caused by the gunshot wound. The inquest into his death was held at the *Dolphin Hotel* in Bootle on the following Tuesday, at which the accused was committed to stand trial for murder. When she appeared before the town's magistrates two days later, she gave a different account of what had happened, and claimed that it had been her husband who had been standing behind her who had fired the gun.

However, although her husband had disappeared after the shooting and had left the seven children to the care of relatives and the workhouse, this claim did not form the basis of her defence at the trial. Her barrister claimed that no evidence had been given that she had loaded the gun or was aware that it was loaded before pointing it at the victim. Her intention in doing so had been merely to frighten him and not kill him. The suggestion that she should be found not guilty and be allowed home to care for her children or that she be convicted of the lesser charge of manslaughter was discounted by the jury. She was sentenced to death after being found guilty of murder.

As the day of the executions approached, it became obvious that there was no public support for a reprieve for Flannigan. However, there was a widespread belief that Mary Williams would be spared, as more information emerged about her victim who had a reputation for violence, and it was felt he had called at her house intending to threaten or possibly harm her.

THE CONDEMNED CRIMINALS

So far, no communication has been received from the Home Office in reference to either of the condemned convicts lying in Kirkdale Gaol under sentence of death. If nothing should be heard to the contrary by noon to-day, the erection of the scaffold will at once be proceeded with, and the executions will take place on Monday morning. It is not yet definitely known upon whom the disagreeable office of executioner will devolve, though it is expected that Calcraft's assistant, who is known to the public by the name of Evans, will perform the duty. It may be remembered that it was he who officiated at the execution of Corrigan, of Chisenhale-street notoriety.

The criminals are both represented as fitly realising their position, and as being perfectly resigned to their fate. Occasionally, however, the wretched woman, Mary Williams, who still adheres to the assertion that it was her husband who fired the fatal shot, gives utterance to a hope that her life may yet be spared. They are both very attentive to the ministrations of Father Bonte, the Roman Catholic chaplain of the prison; and Flanagan often expresses deep contrition for the crime of which he is guilty, maintaining at the same time that he had no intention of murdering his aunt. Neither of the prisoners have been visited by any relatives during the past two days. It is expected that the children of Mary Williams, seven in number, will have a farewell interview with their mother to-day, and a scene of an affecting character is anticipated.

Newspapers printed regular reports on the condemned prisoners. Author's collection

It was also believed by many that despite the evidence pointing to her as the murderer, her husband had been the real culprit and she had been acting to protect him.

A petition on her behalf was organised by Alderman Geves, the Mayor of Bootle, and was signed by all of the members of the jury who had sat at the inquest into her victim. As she awaited the outcome of these efforts on her behalf the condemned woman was permitted to have her three-month-old baby with her. Two days before her scheduled execution all of the children made an emotional visit to the gaol to say their farewells. There was to be no reprieve and a few hours before she was to be hanged her baby was taken away.

The two murderers were hanged simultaneously on the gallows at Kirkdale by William Marwood. As the noose was being placed over her head, Mary said to the assembled journalists that her husband had been responsible for the crime. Her final words were: 'God Bless' to the female warder who had been her escort and who was in an extremely distressed state.

Some of her children were placed with relatives and the eldest, a twelve-year-old daughter, was sent to the local Industrial School; the others, including the three-month-old baby, were sent to the West Derby Workhouse.

William Marwood. Author's collection

CHAPTER 12

Murder by Fire
1879

It was a little after one o'clock in the morning of Sunday 9 November 1879, and Constable Thomas Burrows was walking his beat along Swan Street in Manchester. Suddenly, he saw a flash of light in the upstairs window of number 4, which was immediately followed by the unmistakable sound of a large fire starting. He rushed to the front door, which after a few moments was opened by a boy, who allowed the officer to enter. As he did so Constable Burrows saw thirty-three-year-old Rose Ann Cassidy on the stairs, naked and horribly burnt all over her body. He rushed up to her and helped her to a chair in the downstairs front room.

He ran upstairs once again and was attempting to extinguish the flames when Rose's husband William appeared on the landing. He was fully dressed and the officer urged him to fetch more buckets of water, but William, who said nothing, walked downstairs and into the front room without offering any help. Having put out the fire, the constable made for the front room, where several women, who had come to assist, were tending to Rose. She pointed to her husband, who had still not spoken, and cried out: 'Will, you have done it, you have tried many times, but you have done it at last.'

Rose, accompanied by Constable Burrows, was taken to Manchester Royal Infirmary, and after ensuring she was receiving medical attention, the officer returned to the Cassidy home, where he advised her husband that she had continued to accuse him of setting light to the bed deliberately. He denied this, and when asked why he had not denied the accusation when first made by his wife, he replied: 'Do you think I was going to talk before a lot of women?'

He said he had called at the nearby *Nelson Inn* earlier, and had returned home at eleven o'clock, where he found Rose in a very drunken state. He continued by claiming that she was an alcoholic. They had gone to bed together, but she was so drunk that she kept falling to the floor as she undressed, before she eventually managed to climb into bed. He could not sleep, so dressed and went downstairs where he eventually dozed off in a chair. The next he knew he was being wakened by his son who told him of the fire, and that he had let a policeman into the house. It was then that he went upstairs where he found Constable Burrows trying to put out the flames. Unsure what to do and in a state of shock, he returned downstairs.

Arrangements were made for Rose to make a deposition from her hospital bed, and later that day her husband was taken to the hospital to hear it being made. She stated:

I live at 4 Swan Street off Rochdale Road, and went about half-past ten o'clock to bed. My husband had come home yesterday afternoon from his work, gone out again, and come into tea, which we had together. He went out again about seven o'clock, but I don't know what time he came in.

Constable Burrows was unable to save Rose Ann Cassidy. Illustrated Police News

I believe I was in bed then. I was awakened by being on fire. I then heard my husband going downstairs and called to him but he made no answer. I knew his footstep. No one slept in the room with me. We have no fire in the bedroom, as we use a paraffin lamp. I took it upstairs, but did not put it out, as it always burns low at night. I put the lamp on the floor, where it always stands. When I woke on being on fire, I found the lamp about a yard from the bed, at the front of a box near to the bed. I did not hear anyone in the room between the time I went to bed and the time I found myself burning. The lamp could not possibly have set fire to the bed. When I was burning I went downstairs after my husband. He was sitting on a chair near the fire, and the constable came in before he stirred. He was awake. I had no quarrel with my husband that day, but I had the day before, about some work. He is a clicker for a boot maker. About a fortnight ago I fell asleep with my legs crossed on the fender in front of the fire, and was awakened by being burnt on the foot. My husband said that was a ready way of awakening me. I saw no poker in his hand then, but believe he burnt me with one. I cannot tell how the bed got on fire, but I did say last night that my husband had done it. My husband threatened about three months ago to swing for me, and has said he would kill me. He has beaten me and some time ago kicked me on the eye, and I was under the infirmary about a fortnight.

Cassidy was charged by Superintendent Godby of Goulden Street Police Station, with the attempted murder of his wife. However, following her death at three o'clock on the morning of Monday, the charge was amended to that of murder, and he was subsequently committed to stand trial at the Manchester Assizes. This took place the following January before Lord Justice Brett, with HW West QC and Mr Blair representing the Crown, and he was defended by Mr Nolan and Mr Hindle.

The prosecution opened its case by describing a severe deterioration in the accused's relationship with his wife after thirteen years of marriage. She had told relatives and friends that she had suffered several beatings at his hands, and on a

Manchester Royal Infirmary. Author's collection

number of occasions he had threatened to kill her. Her deposition was read out, which was followed by expert testimony relating to how the fire started.

Superintendent A Tozer of the Manchester Fire Brigade had examined the bed, blankets and mattress in which Rose had suffered her horrific injuries. He had concluded that the top surface of the bedrail furthest from the lamp was more scorched on the top than on the underside, which suggested to him that this had been caused by an inflammable liquid such as paraffin being poured along the top of the rail. On one of the blankets, he discovered two distinct areas where an inflammable liquid had been used to start a fire, and he believed if such a liquid had not been used so liberally, the bed would not have burnt as fiercely as it had.

Analytical chemist, Mr W Thompson, had examined a pillow and a piece of blanket from the scene, which he confirmed had been doused in paraffin. When asked by the defence if he had heard of the practice of paraffin being put on a bed to keep vermin away, he confirmed that he had indeed heard of this.

No witnesses were called by the defence, which relied on the argument that the Crown had not proven its case. It was argued that in her deposition, powerful though it was, Rose could not state categorically that she had seen her husband start the fire. It was also argued that despite the persuasive expert testimony, it had not been proven how the fire started. An alternative scenario was put, and this had been hinted at in the cross-examination of Mr Thompson. It was argued that the paraffin had been put on the bed by Rose to keep away rats and mice when she went to bed; as she undressed, her clothing had been set alight by the lamp; she had rolled on the bed in a desperate attempt to try and put out the flames, which would explain the apparent separate points of ignition.

It was an inspired argument, but after deliberating for ninety minutes the jury found Cassidy guilty of murder, and on being sentenced to death he shouted: 'I know no more of the charge than a child unborn. I am as innocent as William Habron was of the murder of Cock. I know nothing about it. I don't indeed.'

Cassidy was referring to a notorious local miscarriage of justice, when several years earlier, William Habron had been wrongly convicted of murdering a Manchester police officer. He was sentenced to death but later reprieved. In 1879, Charles Peace, one of Victorian England's most famous criminals, had confessed to the crime on the eve of his execution for a different murder, which led to a pardon for William Habron.

Indeed, many believed Cassidy to be innocent of his wife's murder, and others felt that there was sufficient doubt, making a reprieve, for which there was widespread support, inevitable. However, the Home Secretary refused to intervene and Cassidy was hanged at Strangeways Gaol on 17 February 1880.

The execution would prove to be one of the most controversial carried out in Manchester. Reporters had not been allowed to witness the hanging, which was happening more often as the Home Office attempted to prevent the reporting of these events in the press. However, on this occasion the reporters were told they would not be allowed to attend the inquest into Cassidy's death, which in line with custom and practice, was due to be heard in the gaol, shortly after the body was taken down from the gallows.

The local coroner, Frederick Price, disagreed with this decision in the strongest possible terms. As far as he was concerned his court had to be open to the public, but as this was impracticable, he viewed the press as representatives of the general public. Therefore, after he and the jury had viewed Cassidy's body, they left the gaol and accompanied by a group of reporters they made their way to the nearby *Woolsack Hotel*, where the inquest was held.

The jury members had clearly been disturbed at what they had seen when examining Cassidy's body, for he had almost been decapitated. The Deputy Governor of the gaol was pressed on the length of drop used but he could not be certain. A juror suggested it must have been at least nine feet six inches in length, which was far too long. Ironically, the executioner, who by then had left the gaol and was not available to give evidence, was William Marwood. He was a thoughtful, humane and decent man, who had been the first to hold the post of executioner to apply scientific principles to his task. He had developed a method of calculating the length of rope used, based on the height and weight of the condemned. This was so that too short a drop, which would lead to a slow death by strangulation, or too long a drop which would result in decapitation, would be avoided. Nevertheless, it was obvious that Marwood had miscalculated on this occasion.

Following what they had witnessed, the Cassidy jury made it clear that they believed that despite executions being carried out in private, the public should still have a means of knowing what went on behind the closed doors of the hanging shed, and it was therefore crucial that reporters were permitted to witness executions. With the full support of the coroner, the jury forwarded the following recommendation to the Home Secretary: 'The jury begs to express a wish that at future executions reporters of the press should be allowed to be present.'

CHAPTER 13

The Wedding Day Murder
1881

At eight o'clock on the morning of Wednesday 3 August 1881, sixteen-year-old Ann Ratcliffe left her home, the *Blue Bell* on Church Street, Preston, of which her father Alfred was the landlord. It was to be the most wonderful day of her life for she was due to marry her lover and the father of the baby she was expecting in the near future, twenty-one-year-old John Aspinall Simpson. Her father did not know of the arrangements but she had told her sister that John had arranged for the ceremony to take place that morning at St Paul's Church, and as they did not yet have anywhere to live, she would return home alone following the ceremony.

John left his home at about the same time, and told his sister, who knew of the wedding, that she should wait until a friend came to take her to the church. However, there was to be no wedding, and within the hour, Ann would be dead.

He had arranged to meet Ann close to the church, but took her to a public house, the *Sir Walter Scott* on North Street, which they entered at 8.30. They were served with two glasses of lemonade by Mary Quigley, daughter of the landlady, and sat by the window in the best parlour. A few minutes later, Mary looked through the open door and saw the young couple deep in conversation. Ten minutes later, Mary heard the sound of a glass breaking.

Once again, Mary looked into the room and was horrified to see the girl gripping her throat from which blood was pouring onto the floor. Mary ran for her mother, Ann, who was in the yard, and the two women returned to the parlour. They found the girl lying on the hearth rug in front of the fireplace, still bleeding from her wound. The young man was sitting by the window as though in a daze, and made no response when Ann

Ann Ratcliffe fell to the floor holding her throat from which blood was pouring.
Illustrated Police News

screamed: 'What have you done this for?' Mary went in search of a policeman, and Ann asked two men, Joseph Farnworth and William Bradshaw, who happened to be passing the pub, to help.

Joseph found the girl to be still alive, but only just. He turned to Simpson and asked him, 'What have you been doing?' to which he responded, 'I don't know.' After a few moments, the girl stopped breathing and when William told Simpson of this, he replied: 'It's me.' William and Joseph noticed an open razor smeared with blood, on the table, and as they awaited the arrival of the police, the two men held onto Simpson to ensure he could not grab it nor flee.

Constable William Roocroft was the first police officer at the scene, and given the accounts told to him by the landlady and her daughter, together with the fact that there was blood on his hands and clothing, he arrested Aspinall on suspicion of murder. When later charged with the crime he made no reply.

Surgeon Charles Green had arrived at the pub within a matter of minutes and declared the girl dead. He performed a post-mortem soon afterwards, and found a deep wound to her throat, which was four inches long, exposed the spinal column and severed the windpipe, carotid artery, and jugular vein. She had lost a massive amount of blood, and the razor found at the scene was undoubtedly the murder weapon.

Within two hours of her death, an inquest opened at the local police station before the coroner, Mr Gilbertson. Members of the jury were taken to the scene of the crime, after which they visited the mortuary to view the body. On returning to the police station they heard details of the post-mortem and from those who had witnessed the morning's events. Her father provided evidence of identification, together with details of the relationship between his daughter and Simpson. The jury decided that Ann had been murdered at the hands of the suspect already in custody and he was committed to stand trial.

At noon, a little over three hours since the crime was committed, the suspect appeared before the town's magistrates. When he was brought into the dock, bloodstains remained on his hands. Similar evidence to that given before the coroner was heard and following an adjournment of twenty-four hours, he was again committed to stand trial.

When news of Simpson's arrest had become known, there was a sense of shock throughout the town as he belonged to a well known and respected local family. His grandfather was a watch and clock maker, Jonathon Simpson, whose workshop was on Lune Street; and a founding member of the town's temperance movement. Jonathon's son, John, helped in the business and married Mary Aspinall, who gave birth to the murder suspect. Following the early death of John she left the Lune Street premises and opened a grocer's shop on Meadow Street.

As a child, the suspect had been an intelligent and conscientious youngster and after leaving school he worked for a solicitor and also in the office of the District Registrar for Marriages in Preston. However, at the age of nineteen he began associating with bad company, refused to work, and had to be supported by his elderly mother. However, in the more recent past he had assured his family and Ann that he had been offered a well-paid job in Manchester, where he and his bride would be living.

The dead girl's family had moved to Preston from Darwen eight years earlier and at the time the *Blue Bell* was a notorious establishment. However, Alfred and his wife, who died in 1879, transformed it, and the inn was now highly respectable and the landlord was much admired throughout the area. Since her mother's death, Ann had worked for her father and was popular with the customers.

Her relationship with Simpson had begun shortly after her mother had died, when he began frequenting the inn and Ann was just fourteen years of age. Initially, her father refused to believe the rumours of their relationship, and was far from happy as he considered the young man to be a feckless individual. He attempted to prevent him from seeing Ann but they continued to meet in secret and he had to accept the situation.

The murderer, his victim and places associated with the crime. Illustrated Police News

Several of his customers told Alfred that they had seen Ann serving her boyfriend with drinks without taking payment from him. She denied this when confronted, but her father had had enough and barred him from the inn. Nevertheless, the relationship continued and in July 1881, Ann broke the news to her father that she was pregnant. He therefore agreed, albeit reluctantly, that she could marry him, and signed the necessary consent form, which Simpson had provided, having also promised to make all the necessary arrangements.

However, there was to be no joyous wedding ceremony, and instead, Ann's funeral took place on the Saturday morning after her murder. The cortege left the *Blue Bell* at eleven o'clock and a crowd estimated to number 5,000 had gathered in the streets surrounding the inn, and many thousands more lined the route to the cemetery. By the time Ann was in her grave, the police had amassed a considerable amount of information, which it was believed demonstrated that this had been a cold, callous and clearly premeditated crime, for which a motive could also be shown.

The dead girl's sister, Edith, disclosed that Ann had been expecting to marry the accused on Monday 2 August and had met him at 7 30 in the morning, at the *King's Arms*, but the ceremony had not taken place. Simpson had insisted at the time that he had arranged for the ceremony to take place, and could not understand why the registrar had not turned up. Simpson had gone to the official's home and he assured Ann that he had been informed that it was not convenient to conduct the marriage ceremony that day and the Registrar had refused to leave his home. Ann had been inconsolable but calmed down when Simpson promised to make alternative arrangements, so they might marry forty-eight hours later.

However, George Dixon, the local Registrar of Marriages informed the police that Simpson had failed to hand in the form signed by Ann's father, consenting to the marriage. Roger Kenyon, the verger of St Paul's Church confirmed that no arrangements had been made for the supposed wedding ceremony. To the police, this information confirmed that Simpson had no intention of marrying the girl.

Barber Samuel Weights reported that the accused man had called at his shop at 11.30 on the Saturday night before the murder, asking for a shave. After he had left the premises, Samuel noticed that one of his three identical cut-throat razors was missing, and he suspected Simpson of taking it. It was this razor, identified by the maker's name it bore on the blade, John Heiffor, 3 Paradise Square, Sheffield, that was later used as the murder weapon.

Emily Richardson was a former girlfriend of the accused and she had met him several months before the crime. She had asked him if he intended marrying Ann, to which he replied: 'To Hell with marriage. I am only after the cash bag there.' Thomas Jackson, who knew the dead girl and the accused, worked on Back Grimshaw Street. He had seen the couple regularly over several months and he recalled one conversation he overheard when Simpson said to her: 'Have you got any money?' to which she replied: 'No, do you think I can always be robbing my father for you?'

This supported her father's suspicion that his daughter had in the past been stealing money from the till to give to Simpson, but in recent weeks she had stopped doing so. With that source of income closed to him, he had, it was assumed, decided to murder her. That he should choose to do so in a public place and remain at the scene was initially difficult to make any sense of. However, he later produced a letter she had written to him in the past threatening to kill herself if he should leave her. He now claimed that she had produced the razor and used it to kill herself after he had told her the wedding would not be taking place and he was ending the relationship.

The trial took place at Manchester Assizes on Monday 7 November 1881 before Mr Justice Kay. The Crown's case was put by Mr Shree, who urged the jury not to be fooled by the prisoner's claim that Ann had committed suicide. Mr Foard, for the defence, argued that the evidence against his client was circumstantial, and his client's version of events could not be disproved.

Mr Foard was particularly scathing in his description of Emily Richardson's evidence, which was of course very damaging to his client. He claimed that she was keen to gain revenge on Simpson for ending their relationship and becoming involved with Ann. Simpson's barrister also attempted to explain why when asked at the scene immediately after Ann had died, who had been responsible, he had replied "It's me". He insisted that this was not a confession as it was being portrayed by the Crown, but an expression of his accepting some responsibility for her decision to commit suicide.

Having listened to the judge's summing up of the evidence, the jury took just twenty-five minutes to find Simpson guilty of murder. When asked if he had anything to say before sentence of death was passed, Simpson replied: 'No Sir, I am perfectly satisfied.' The judge told Simpson that he agreed fully with the verdict and that he should not expect a reprieve.

An attempt to obtain a reprieve for Simpson was abandoned after a petition gained only a handful of signatures. As he awaited his execution, Simpson asked his sister Lizzie to approach Ann's father to ask if he would visit him in Strangeways Gaol. Despite Lizzie's reservations, she was met with a great deal of warmth by the grieving father, who expressed his regrets that she and her elderly mother had suffered so much as a result of Simpson's crime. He decided against visiting the condemned man, but asked Lizzie to let him know that he forgave him. Furthermore, he wanted him to know that he bore no ill-will towards his relatives, and he hoped that their shared experiences of this tragedy would lead to a lasting friendship between the two families.

Simpson had a photograph of Ann in the condemned cell, which he asked the authorities for permission to have it buried with him. However, shortly before his execution, which was carried out by William Marwood on Monday 28 November 1881, he learnt that his request had been refused. The governor had refused the press permission to witness the execution, but journalists were allowed to attend the inquest held later in the prison.

CHAPTER 14

The Cornermen
1884

It was twenty minutes to eleven on the night of Saturday 5 January 1884 when Constable Edward Evans noticed a crowd had gathered at the Lancaster and Yorkshire Railway Bridge on Blackstone Street in Liverpool. He walked over to investigate and found spreadeagled on the ground, what he first of all thought was a foreign-looking and drunken seaman. He called for a wheelbarrow to take him to the Collingwood Dock Bridewell, but realised that the man had in fact suffered stab wounds. The constable arranged for him to be taken by ambulance to the Northern Hospital where he was pronounced dead on arrival by Dr Francis Johnston.

There were a number of witnesses to the events leading to the still unidentified man's death. He had been walking towards the docks with another foreign-looking sailor when they were attacked by a gang of five youths on the corner of Blackstone Street. Known locally as 'cornermen', such gangs had been responsible for a number of unprovoked attacks in the area in the preceding months. Speaking to the witnesses revealed that the two men had been beaten, knocked to the ground and kicked before being struck with belts. One of the gang's victims had managed to run away before he had suffered serious injuries, but his companion had not been so fortunate. The witnesses were able to provide the police with descriptions and in some cases the names of the alleged attackers.

As a result of this information the police searched a number of empty houses in the area in the early hours of Sunday morning which were believed to be used as shelters by the gang. In one of these, at 41 Fulton Street, an eighteen-year-old labourer named Michael McLean was arrested. When searched he was found to be in possession of three knives and a belt with a large heavy buckle. McLean was already wanted by the police for questioning, as he was thought to have robbed a woman of a large amount of money after throwing pepper in her face some days earlier.

Over the following two days four other suspects were detained and these were Patrick Duggan, an eighteen-year-old scaler; Murdoch 'Mooney' Ballantyne, a twenty-year-old labourer; nineteen-year-old labourer William Dempsey; and twenty-year-old barber Alexander Campbell. All five were charged with murder.

The dead man had suffered three stab wounds but the fatal one was to the lower part of his neck, close to the collar bone. It was very deep and had almost entered his chest, having caused considerable internal damage and an excessive loss of blood.

Despite the arrests the police still had no idea who the victim was. However, on the Monday following the crime, Patrick Coulter came forward to identify the body as that of Michael Mellet, one of his lodgers, who had left his house on Saturday night and had not returned. The lodging house keeper proved to be wrong and two days later the dead man's true identity became known.

The deceased was twenty-six-year-old Spanish seaman Exeguiel Rodriguez Nunez, mate on the steamer *Serra*, which had arrived in the port from Havana on Saturday morning and which was anchored in the Huskisson Dock. The identification was provided by a compatriot, Jose Jiminez, a sailor on another Spanish ship, the *Magaellanea*, which was in the Canada Dock. He was the man who had been attacked with his friend on the previous Saturday night, but who had been able to escape.

He explained that he had not come forward earlier as in his homeland severe restrictions were imposed on the movements of any witness to a murder and he had feared the same applied in this country. It was after being reassured that this was not the case that he had approached the police.

The trial of the five accused began on 18 February, with the Crown opening its case by claiming that the men subjected the

Canada Dock. Liverpool Central Library

two Spanish sailors to a brutal and unprovoked attack and the deceased was the victim of a senseless and motiveless crime.

Jose Jiminez testified that he was punched in the face by Ballantyne, but escaped before he suffered any further injuries. This meant he did not see what happened to his friend, but there were a number of witnesses to what did happen to him. Esther Ramsey and Esther Conbey saw McLean and Duggan chase him. When they had caught up with him they knocked him to the ground and beat him with their belts, after which Duggan was heard to shout: 'Mooney, Mooney, I have done it.'

Several children also witnessed the assault, most of whom told the police that McLean and Duggan had taken leading roles. Fourteen-year-old Annie Killan and eleven-year-old Margaret Killery also told of seeing Campbell and Dempsey catching hold of the seaman, kicking him and beating him with their belts. Margaret also heard Campbell shout: 'Knives boys, knives.' Twelve-year-old Georgina Ballantyne, sister of one of the accused, witnessed these events, although she testified that her brother had taken no part in the assault after she pleaded with him not to become involved.

John Hodge and Peter Burke, both eleven years of age, swore that they heard Campbell shout: 'Give me a knife, my belt's broke', and shortly afterwards: 'I've done him.' Fourteen-year-old Katherine Burke saw Constable Evans approaching the scene and heard McLean shout to his friends: 'Here's a bobby, let's run', after which the five young men walked calmly away from the scene.

However, the most damaging testimony as far as Duggan and McLean were concerned, was that provided by thirteen-year-old Hugh Callaghan, who told of seeing those two stab their victim as he lay helpless on the ground.

The Crown's case was obviously strong and managed to place all of the defendants at the scene of the crime. However, the defence barristers began by warning the jury not to send five young men to their deaths on the gallows on the evidence of children.

Also of significance was the revelation that emerged for the first time at the trial during the evidence of Inspector Pegler, one of the senior investigating officers. He revealed that Nunez had a knife concealed in his clothing. This had not been stated at the coroner's or magistrates' hearings, and the defendants' barristers claimed this demonstrated that the evidence of the police was tainted and should be ignored. It also provided an opportunity to open a new line of defence, for it was now claimed that Campbell had shouted: 'Knives, boys, knives', not with the intention of encouraging his friends to use theirs, but warning them that Nunez had one.

The Crown argued that the knife had only been discovered when the deceased's clothing was being removed prior to the post-mortem and could not possibly have been produced beforehand by Nunez. The judge supported this viewpoint in his summing up, and advised the jury that claims of acting in self-defence were not available to the defendants.

The jury took under an hour to reach their verdicts. Campbell, Dempsey and Ballantyne were acquitted but McLean and Duggan were convicted of wilful murder, but this was accompanied by a strong recommendation for mercy for both of them.

When asked if there was a reason why the death sentence should not be passed, McLean replied: 'I am innocent of the charge. The prisoner Dempsey who has now been discharged is guilty of the murder of the man.' Duggan responded similarly by claiming: 'I am innocent of the charge. Dempsey is the man who committed the murder.'

Having placed the black cap on his head, the judge, obviously taking account of Liverpool's position as one of the world's leading ports told them:

> You have been found guilty of the wilful murder of a very savage character. It would indeed be a scandal if it could be said that foreigners visiting our shores, passing inoffensively along the streets of our towns, might be hunted to death with impunity. The jury have strongly recommended you to the mercy of the court and it will be my duty to forward the recommendation to those with whom the decision rests.

Petitions were organised but only Duggan was reprieved.

There was a heavy fall of snow on the morning of McLean's execution on 10 March. A crowd of 500 gathered outside Kirkdale Gaol, among them his sister who had covered her head with a shawl, and his girlfriend who wore crape in her bonnet. They were stood with a group of relatives and neighbours, but his parents had decided not to attend.

Inside the gaol, Father Bonte administered the last rites at seven o'clock after which McLean ate breakfast. The hangman, Bartholomew Binns, pinioned his arms shortly before eight, after which McLean ran nimbly up the steps of the scaffold. As his knees were being strapped together McLean turned to the journalists who had been admitted to witness the execution, and said:

> Gentlemen, I consider it a disgrace to the police force of Liverpool and to the laws of the country that I am going to suffer death and another boy imprisoned for life for a crime of which we are both innocent, as God is my judge.

These were his last words.

Usually, the inquest into the death of an executed prisoner was a formality, but this was not the case on this occasion. The governor of the gaol, Major Leggatt, had witnessed Binns at work previously and had not been impressed. Unbeknown to Binns, the major was given permission by Lancashire's Sheriff to invite Samuel Heath to act as assistant at the hanging.

Clearly, the Major's worries were not misplaced for Binns arrived at the gaol on Saturday afternoon drunk and was abusive and threatening towards prison staff. It was only after Major Legatt threatened to call for the police that the executioner calmed down. When Heath arrived on the following day, Binns was outraged and refused to associate with him or allow him to assist at the hanging.

Regrettably, the execution did not pass without incident, and the surgeon reported that McLean's heart continued to beat for thirteen minutes after he had fallen through the drop. When Binns attempted to leave the gaol after the hanging, he was refused permission do to so and was compelled to attend the inquest. Witnesses claimed he had placed the eyelet of the noose in the wrong place and calculated the drop incorrectly.

Having found that McLean had been killed lawfully the jury foreman continued by telling the coroner:

> We have agreed Sir, that we think Binns deserving severe censure for the manner in which he carried out the execution. He appears to have no scientific principle for going through his work, and we think this really requires a scientific man. He seems to have no system.

Binns would not take the leading role at an execution again, and it was not until the early years of the twentieth century that he was allowed to act as an assistant.

On the day of McLean's execution, it was reported in the local press that Dempsey had sailed for San Francisco to begin a new life in California.

CHAPTER 15

A Murder in the Workhouse
1887

Walton Gaol opened in the mid nineteenth century and the first hanging took place behind its walls with the execution of Elizabeth Berry. This meant that for a few years Liverpool had two hanging prisons. The last to take place in Kirkdale Gaol was in August 1891, after which all executions would take place at Walton.

Following the deaths of her husband and son, Elizabeth Berry arranged for her then six-year-old daughter, Edith Annie, to live with the girl's aunt, Ann Sanderson, and her husband, at 68 Hermin Street, Miles Platting in Manchester. Elizabeth paid her sister-in-law three shillings weekly for her

Elizabeth Berry. Jo Carlon

food and an additional sixpence towards her education. Edith's life was insured for £13 with the Rational Assurance Company and Ann paid the one penny weekly premiums, which Elizabeth, the beneficiary, reimbursed quarterly.

Elizabeth continued to play an active role in her daughter's upbringing, but the arrangement allowed Elizabeth to take up several nursing positions to support Edith and herself. In July 1886, she took up such a post at the Oldham Workhouse, at an annual salary of £25. As Christmas approached it was agreed that Edith would stay in Miles Platting but spend a few days over the New Year period with her mother in her private quarters at the workhouse, and take her thirteen-year-old friend Beatrice Hall with her.

The girls arrived in Oldham on Wednesday 29 December and that night the excited youngsters shared Elizabeth's bed. On Thursday, the girls were allowed out and gorged themselves on cocoa nut chips and chocolate. The next day they visited the market where they bought fish for their supper, which once again both of them ate. Edith also bought a brooch for her mother.

Edith posted a letter to her aunt and uncle which they received on New Year's Eve, in which she wrote excitedly of how much fun she and Beatrice were having and how wonderful her mother had looked when she dressed for a dance that was held in the workhouse.

Edith and Beatrice rose early on Saturday, New Years Day and were seen by a number of people who noticed that they seemed well and in high spirits. A little later however, Edith became ill and began to vomit, which was streaked with blood. There had been no improvement by late morning which led Elizabeth to call for Dr Patterson, the workhouse medical officer, who although he did not live on site, came immediately he received word of Edith being unwell.

He arrived to find Edith lying on the sofa in front of the fire in her mother's room. She vomited a number of times during his stay and complained of stomach pains. Given the symptoms, he believed her to be suffering from an ulcerated stomach and prescribed a solution of bicarbonate of soda and creosote. Dr Patterson visited again on Saturday night, and although there had been no improvement in her condition, he suggested that a good night's sleep would do her good. Seeing that Elizabeth was very tired, Ellen Thompson, an assistant nurse, offered to sit with Edith throughout the night, but her mother declined this thoughtful and kind offer from her colleague.

On Sunday morning, Edith appeared to be much improved and Dr Patterson told her mother that there was a very good chance that her daughter would recover. He thought the internal bleeding was probably due to a ruptured stomach, which was not uncommon in young girls. He left saying he would return that evening to check on her progress.

That afternoon, Mary Jane Knight, one of Elizabeth's inmate servants visited Edith and spent several hours with her. She would later recall that the only thing her mother gave her to either eat or drink was a cup of tea, which Mary Jane also drank. She described it as tasting rather good. Nevertheless, Edith's condition deteriorated and another member of staff, Lydia Evitt, who visited Edith, was the first to notice that red marks had appeared around her mouth and on her lips. When

Edith Berry. Jo Carlon

she commented on this, Elizabeth said: 'See what the orange has done to Edith's mouth', and explained she had given her daughter a slice of orange a little earlier.

When Dr Patterson arrived on Sunday night, Edith's condition had deteriorated badly. She had a weak pulse, her eyes were sunken, and the pain had spread from her stomach to the whole of her abdomen. Elizabeth told the doctor that Edith had been 'purged' and her evacuations contained blood. The doctor also noticed the swelling and stains around her mouth, and on this occasion Elizabeth said it was because she had given the girl lemon and sugar.

Dr Patterson decided to seek a second opinion and Dr Robertson came to Elizabeth's quarters at 11.30pm. It was decided to change her medication to a mixture of bismuth and morphia, but before leaving, Dr Patterson warned Elizabeth that Edith was in a dangerous condition, and might not survive the night. Nevertheless, at this stage he did not mention to her his belief that after leaving Edith earlier that morning, she had been given poison.

Edith's condition did deteriorate, and soon after she had received her niece's letter saying what a wonderful time she was having with her mother, her aunt received a telegram from her sister-in-law which read simply: 'Come at once. Annie is dying'. Her aunt and uncle managed to spend a few hours with Edith before her death at five o'clock in the morning on Tuesday 4 January. Dr Patterson issued a death certificate giving the cause as acute inflammation of the mucous membrane of the stomach and bowels.

However, he did so only after sharing his concerns with the police, who agreed to this course of action so that Edith could be buried, but not before a post-mortem was conducted and her internal organs had been removed for examination. He had told them that the dead girl's mother was the only person apart from himself to have a key to the dispensary. She did not have a key to the poisons cabinet, but as he had no reason to be suspicious of her, she was often left alone in the room with the cupboard open and would have had access to the poisons.

Dr Patterson examined the girl's body but could find no evidence of poison, other than a trace of sulphuric acid, but this was not a large enough amount to kill her. He had still not told Elizabeth of his suspicions when he sent the internal organs to Manchester's analyst, Charles Estcort.

On 6 January, Elizabeth was interviewed by the police regarding the issues that had been raised by Dr Patterson. She seemed unperturbed and explained that her daughter had been suffering from constipation when she collected her at Miles Platting, and her sister-in-law had told her that when she had given Edith a pill, she always passed blood. Elizabeth concluded by referring to Edith's inflamed mouth by saying: 'Before she died her mouth was ulcerated and I suppose that must be the cause.' The interviewing officer asked: 'As a nurse you must have seen many children after death, but have you ever seen a mouth like that before?' She confirmed that she had not and suddenly became agitated and cried out: 'Why should I have killed my darling? I had just doubled my insurance for her benefit in the Prudential.'

However, subsequent enquiries by the police confirmed that they had been lied to. Edith's aunt insisted that she had not been suffering from constipation, had not been given any pills, and had not passed blood before visiting her mother in the workhouse.

It was also established that neither Edith nor her mother were insured with the Prudential. The police did learn however, from James Pickford, secretary of the Rational Sick and Burial Society, that Elizabeth had received £10, the sum for which Edith's life had been insured, two days after her death. Her lies and receipt of the insurance money did not lead to her immediate arrest as the police awaited the results of the examination of the dead girl's organs.

Mr Estcort had received Edith's organs four days after her death and they contained the stomach and its contents, her large and small intestines, parts of her spleen, liver, right kidney, gullet, part of her duodenum and a piece of her liver. He found a little sulphuric acid, the presence of which might have been due to natural causes, but could find no evidence of any poison that might have contributed to her death.

Nevertheless, he testified at the inquest that in some circumstances, especially when there is a great deal of vomiting, the residue of any poison could leave the body. He supported the findings of Drs Patterson and Robertson that the cause of death was due to the administration of poison.

The inquest had not been completed but Elizabeth was arrested on 13 January on suspicion of having poisoned Edith and was held in custody. One week later, having heard Mr Estcort's findings, the coroner's jury returned a verdict of wilful murder and named Elizabeth as the killer.

The alleged murderer still had to appear before the town's magistrates and did so on 27 January. Her defence team put forward a powerful argument on her behalf, describing her as a gentlewoman of unimpeachable character, and pouring scorn on the Crown's argument that she would murder her beloved daughter for £10 insurance money. It was pointed out for instance that at no time during Edith's stay at the workhouse, did Elizabeth attempt to prevent anyone visiting the girl, and indeed several members of staff had sat with her for varying lengths of time. None of these people had been suspicious nor had they witnessed any uncaring attitude towards her daughter.

Furthermore, none of those who saw Edith after she fell ill heard her complain about anything her mother had done to her or given her to eat or drink. Elizabeth had made no attempt to conceal the bloodstained vomit, and it was she who had called for Dr Patterson to visit her daughter. It was also argued that if the doctor came to suspect foul play by the Sunday evening, why had he not taken steps to at least try and remove the girl from her mother's care. It was also emphasised that there was no evidence of the presence of any substantial amount of poison that might have killed her.

The magistrates retired for fifteen minutes and on their return acquitted the defendant. The verdict was met by much applause and cheering in the courtroom, for she had many supporters who were convinced of her innocence. A defence fund was set up on her behalf for she still had to face trial on the coroner's warrant. It was now too late for her to attend the next Manchester Assizes, and she was therefore transferred to Walton Gaol to await her appearance before the Liverpool Assizes. She was in the unusual position of being named as her daughter's murderer at the inquest but cleared by Oldham's magistrates.

The publicity surrounding the events at Oldham Workhouse led to the Rochdale police re-investigating the death of Elizabeth's mother, fifty-eight-year-old Mary Ann Finley. She had died at her home, 4 Albion Street, Castleton on Saturday 13 February 1886, after a brief illness. At the time she was being cared for by Elizabeth who had moved in with her a fortnight earlier. Mary was popular in the district and had several close friends who had been suspicious at the time of her death, but the police did not have enough evidence to initiate a full investigation.

One of these friends was Sarah Ann Wolfenden who was having a cup of tea with Elisabeth shortly after arrival. She told Sarah that she had had a premonition that her mother would die soon, but Sarah reassured her that Mary was in excellent health. Sarah called to see Mary on 12 February, a Friday, and found her to be in good health. On the Saturday morning, however, when she called again she found Mary in a very poor state. She was twitching badly, was having difficulty in breathing, and her tongue was hanging out of her mouth. A short time later, she was dead. A death certificate was issued and she was buried in Moston Cemetery, Manchester. Within days, Elizabeth had sold off her mother's clothing and property, and left the area.

The new investigation led to the police discovering that local chemist John Taylor of Yorkshire Street in Rochdale remembered Elizabeth calling at his shop on two occasions in February 1886. She had bought a total of one and a half ounces of sulphate of atropia, but had used the name Ellen Saunders of Castleton when signing the poisons book. She had assured the chemist that she was a nurse and would be careful when using it as she knew it was a deadly poison.

The police also discovered that Mary's life had been insured with her daughter named as sole beneficiary, with two companies. Frederick Wallwork, district agent for the Wesleyan and General Assurance Society confirmed her life had been insured for £100, and Harry Jackson of the Prudential Assurance Society advised them that Mary's life had been insured for £27 6s.

Given the new information that had been uncovered, the Rochdale coroner opened an inquest into Mary's death, and her body was exhumed. However, the inquest could not be completed before her trial for the murder of Edith as the results of the examination of her internal organs were not yet available. It was therefore adjourned until after the trial at Liverpool, which opened on Monday 21 February 1887 before Mr Justice Hawkins. After all the evidence had been heard, the judge told the jury to focus on two questions: did Edith die as a result of being poisoned? and if so, was the poison administered by her mother?

The jury retired for twelve minutes, before returning with a guilty verdict. The black cap having been placed on his head, Justice Hawkins told the convicted woman:

> The law of this country knows but one punishment for the crime of murder, the crime of which the jury has just now found you guilty. A murder so cold blooded, so merciless and so cruel in causing a poor little child, whom you gave birth to, to suffer so much pain and so much agony, passes all belief". After sentence, she was returned to Walton Gaol.

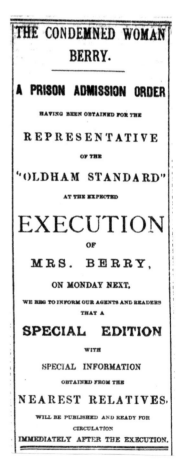

When the inquest into Mary's death resumed in late February, Dr Frank Paul, lecturer in medical jurisprudence at Liverpool University College, confirmed that he had examined the dead woman's internal organs and he was convinced she had been poisoned by atropia. This, together with the other evidence uncovered by the police, led the jury to name Elizabeth as the murderer of her mother. However, given that she was already in the condemned cell, it was

An advertisement for a forthcoming Special Edition on the execution. Oldham Standard

decided to take no further action, and she was not formally charged with the crime.

Further enquiries revealed that Elizabeth had also insured the lives of her husband, Thomas, and had received £18 4s when he died, and she had received £5 insurance on the death of her son Harold, who, like his father, had died some years earlier.

Meanwhile, her solicitor, Joseph Whitaker of 1 St Peter Street, Oldham started a petition hoping to gain a reprieve. Elizabeth still had a good deal of local support as many were not convinced by what was regarded as largely circumstantial evidence against her. Nevertheless, the Home Secretary declined to intervene.

The scaffold on which she would die was being erected in a room immediately below her cell. She became so distressed on being able to hear the workmen going about their business that Mr JM Anderson, the governor of the gaol, arranged for her to be moved to another cell so that she would no longer be disturbed by the work in progress. This was to be the first execution at the gaol and the new gallows with its drop at ground level over a pit ten feet deep, meant the condemned was not required to climb any steps, which could often be a terrible ordeal that prolonged an already distressing process,

and not just for the condemned person, but also those witnessing the event.

Elizabeth Berry was executed on Monday 14 March by James Berry, who had met her at a police ball in Manchester several years earlier, at which they had danced together. They recognised each other and exchanged a few private words before he hanged her.

James Berry who executed his namesake and former dance partner. Author's collection

CHAPTER 16

A Good Citizen is Rewarded
1893

It was almost seven o'clock on the night of Saturday 28 October 1893, when William Denison, who lived at 25 London Street, Salford, heard a loud noise coming from number 23, the home of his neighbour, seventy-four-year-old widow Catherine Tyrer. William was concerned for her well being as he thought she may have fallen and injured herself. His wife went to Catherine's front door and William headed towards the back door, but the house was in darkness.

Another neighbour, Sophia Wilson, who lived at number 21, had also heard the noise and came out to investigate and joined Mrs Denison. She knocked on the front door and a man shouted: 'What do you want in my house?' Within a few seconds, William, who had remained at the rear of the property, saw a stranger emerge from the yard of Catherine's house, and was immediately suspicious, despite the man insisting he now lived there. The stranger ran off with William in pursuit and, following a chase, William grabbed hold of him in a stable yard in West Park Street. There was a struggle, during which William saw the man pull a knife from his pocket, but he managed to disarm him, and throw him to the ground.

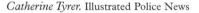

Catherine Tyrer. Illustrated Police News

The scullery, where the murder took place. Illustrated Police News

Back at London Street, Rose Jane Atkins, who lived at number 19, had entered Catherine's house, and had found the elderly woman lying on the scullery floor. Her dress had been pulled above her head, which when pulled away revealed several head wounds from which blood was pouring. She was moving but in great pain, and arrangements were made to take her to Salford Royal Hospital.

The police took the suspect to Trafford Road Police Station and he was quickly identified as Victor Emmanuel Hamer, a twenty-five-year-old house-painter, who lived with his parents on Smith Street. He was known to the police as he had several convictions for dishonesty and in 1881 he had been sentenced to five years in Reformatory School for theft. He had been released from a prison sentence only four months earlier. When asked to explain his presence in the widow's house he replied: 'I will tell you nothing.' When charged with assaulting her he said: 'You can charge me with what you like. It will have to be

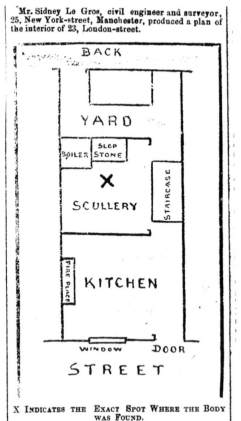

Mr. Sidney Le Gros, civil engineer and surveyor, 25, New York-street, Manchester, produced a plan of the interior of 23, London-street.

A plan of the interior of the victim's home, prepared for the trial. Author's Collection

X INDICATES THE EXACT SPOT WHERE THE BODY WAS FOUND.

proved yet.' Catherine recovered consciousness briefly on Sunday, but died at 6.20 on Monday morning, without having been able to give an account of what had happened to her.

The inquest into her death was held on Tuesday 31 October at the Brotherton Liberal Club, before local coroner, Mr F Price. The body was formally identified by Richard Haselgrove, who was executor to James Tyrer, Catherine's late husband, who had died the previous November. James had been a joiner specialising in making staircases, and Richard had worked with him for many years. They had become close friends and he therefore knew Catherine well and was able to provide the hearing with details of her financial position and her background.

A native of Hull, she had moved to the North West with her husband thirty years earlier. They had no children, but at the time of their marriage James had been a widower with a daughter, who together with Catherine's niece, had kept in contact with her. She was five feet tall, and at the time she was killed was in good health and very active. James had asked Richard to guide her financially, and he kept the promise he made to his old friend by visiting her weekly to not simply give her the money she needed, but also to ensure all was well. She was not wealthy, and in her will she instructed Richard to pay all her outstanding debts, and he was to receive what remained. This meant that Richard was the sole beneficiary but he was never a suspect as the most he would receive would total only a few pounds.

Medical evidence was given by Charles Sutton, Acting Junior House Surgeon at Salford Royal Hospital. On her admission he had treated a massive head wound and a number of facial injuries, but she could not be saved. He performed a post-mortem, and upon opening her head, he had discovered a large skull fracture which was the cause of death. He ruled out the possibility that the injuries had been self-inflicted.

He had to concede that there was a remote possibility that the injuries had been caused by a fall. However, he believed that a great deal of force had been used and that the blows had been delivered during a vicious assault by an attacker. He had found a large lump of coal covered in blood at the scene which he believed was the murder weapon.

The coroner's jury agreed with this version of events and found that Catherine had been murdered by Hamer, who was committed to stand trial at the following Manchester Assizes. This was also the finding when he appeared before the local magistrates.

Hamer's trial was held on Wednesday 8 November 1893 at Manchester, before Mr Justice Grantham. The Crown's case was put by Mr Fleming, and Mr Roe-Rycroft represented the defendant. Despite Catherine being discovered with her lower garments pulled above her waist, a sexual motive was not considered, as it was believed the accused was searching for money hidden in her clothing.

The murderer. Illustrated Police News

It emerged that Hamer had met Catherine a few days before her death. The outsides of the houses on London Street were being painted, and he had been one of the painters hired. One of his workmates, Thomas Jackson, testified that on 24 October Catherine had brewed a pot of tea for them. Hamer and the elderly woman did not get on well from the start and she told him: 'I don't like you', and when asked why this was so she replied: 'Because you are so rough spoken.' This, the Crown suggested, meant that he harboured a grudge against her and had decided to take his revenge.

Catherine's neighbour, Mrs Atkins told the court that she had several conversations with the painters, including Hamer, and asked him if he was married. He replied: 'No damned fear. I am after some married woman or else some old woman.' This, the Crown believed, indicated that a criminal plan was beginning to form in Hamer's mind. The motive was thought to be robbery although a purse containing seven shillings and a few coppers was found on her when she was undressed on arrival at the hospital. Furthermore, Richard Haselgrove had searched the house at the request of the police and having checked his inventory of her possessions, he confirmed that nothing was missing. However, Hamer had been disturbed almost as soon as Catherine was struck and he had little opportunity of making a search. It was thought that the disarranged clothing meant that he had had little time to make a thorough search of her person or the house.

The defence had little alternative other than to acknowledge the presence of their client in the house when Catherine met her death, and faced a difficult task in persuading the jury of his innocence. Nevertheless, they highlighted the possibility that the injuries she suffered might have been caused accidentally and emphasised the fact that no definite motive had been established by the Crown as nothing had been taken from the crime scene.

From the time of his arrest Hamer had claimed that he had been drunk when Catherine died, although this was disputed by the police. However, Thomas Jackson, testified that between midday and five o'clock on the day in question, he had been drinking with Hamer in a number of public houses in Salford, and the accused had drunk eight or nine pints of beer. The defence suggested that Hamer may have struck Catherine, causing her to fall to the floor, and as she did so she may have struck her head on the lump of coal. Given her age and fragile state it would have killed her and the jury should convict Hamer of manslaughter.

The capture of Hamer by William Denison and the death sentence being passed.
Illustrated Police News

In his summing up the judge acknowledged that the jury might understandably have difficulty in accepting that any ill-feeling he felt because Catherine had said she did not like him, or his comments about wishing to find an elderly widow, were proof that he murdered her. Nevertheless, the judge believed they were significant as they did point to what he termed the accused's 'low class of character'. The jury took just under an hour to convict Hamer of murder, after which he was sentenced to death.

There was little public sympathy for Hamer, but he desperately sought a reprieve, which he urged his parents to pursue, for he wrote:

> Dear Mother and Father,
> I now pen these few lines to you to ask you if you will try to do a little bit towards getting me a reprieve, for the time is getting short now, and I think that if you made an effort to do so it may not be too late … Dear Mother, I shall be looking at the door every day now, expecting someone coming to give me some hope, or with the fatal words that I have to die. But I am very glad to say that I am striving to the very uttermost to make my peace with God and to ask his forgiveness for my past life, and I am trusting in his promise that he will do so. I only wish that I had my time to go over again, but of course it is the will of God. I hope you will excuse this short letter, but I cannot express my feelings in words as my head seems confused. Give my best love to all enquiring friends and to my relatives.
> From your loving and most repentant son,
> Emmanuel Hamer

However, there was to be no reprieve, and his execution was fixed for Tuesday 28 November. In his final days there were highly emotional meetings with his parents and other family members, and he wrote his last letter to his sweetheart, Agnes McCulloch. On the eve of his execution, he was visited by Mr Beales, the Superintendent of the Primitive Methodist Sunday School, where the condemned man had been a scholar. Mr Beales later described Hamer as being broken in spirit and resigned to his fate. During the visit Hamer confessed to him, saying:

> I have not told you all. I did it. I remember striking her down. But oh, you do not think I could have done it but for the drink. Oh no, I could not. I had been drinking all week at nights, and on Saturday I had no food, but went at noon to the public house, drinking until I was mad.

As he stood on the gallows, and the hangman James Billington was pulling the white cap down over his face, Hamer uttered his last words, saying in a trembling voice: 'I hope you will forgive me.'

At the inquest into Catherine's death, the coroner had indicated a willingness to recognise William Denison for his crucial part in the capture of the murderer, but stated that he did not have the power to do so. At the conclusion of his trial, and after he had been taken from the dock, the Crown lawyers asked the judge to order a monetary award to the public-spirited neighbour of Hamer's victim. The judge did not believe that he had the power to authorise a reward but said: 'I am prepared to run a little risk however, and in acknowledgement of Denison's promptitude to direct the Sheriff to pay him the sum of two guineas.'

The citizens of Salford believed this to be insufficient, and following the receipt of several letters of support for a more substantial reward, the *Salford Reporter* opened a subscription fund. This received a great deal of support and on Saturday 23 December, at the Salford Police Court, the mayor, Alderman Bailey, presented him with a marble clock and a large cash sum.

CHAPTER 17

Murder on Platform A
1908

Since the first railway murder which was committed by Franz Muller in 1864 the perpetrators of such crimes took advantage of an otherwise empty carriage on a moving train to rob or rape and then kill a passenger. However, the murder discussed in this chapter is wholly different in that the train was stationery and there were several other passengers in the carriage at the time.

At about five o'clock in the evening of Monday 25 May 1908 Constable George Hebden of the Great Central Railway Company noticed a couple arguing on London Road Station, Manchester. A few minutes later, a carriage cleaner told him he was needed urgently on Platform A. When he reached the platform he found a crowd had gathered and he was advised that a man had stabbed a woman, thought to be his wife, after which the man had attempted to cut his own throat. The incident had taken place in a carriage of the 5.20pm train to Glossop. The police officer pushed his way through the crowd and discovered the woman lying on the platform severely wounded. He arranged for her to be taken to Manchester Royal Infirmary but she died on the way there.

Constable Hebden found the man's wound to be superficial and he was taken to Whitworth Street Police Station. On arrival he told the police officers: 'It was all through her not giving me one and sixpence, so that I could go to Blackpool and get work, and she having all that money on her.' Initially, he refused to give his name or details of his victim but documents found on her identified her as forty-three-year-old Ellen Ann Ballington. It was quickly established that the detained man was her forty-one-year-old husband Fred. Later that night at about eight o'clock, he was told of her death and was charged with her murder, to which he replied: 'Murder. Is

London Road Station. Manchester Central Library

she dead? The sooner they hang me the better, then I shall follow her and be with her.' When also charged with attempted suicide he replied simply: 'No.'

Samuel, the son of Ellen and Fred, provided the police with details of his parents' troubled relationship. A native of Derby, his father moved to Glossop six years earlier to work for a master butcher but opened his own shop some time later, in which he was helped by his wife and son. However, the marriage was not a happy one, due mainly to his father's heavy drinking, which led to a number of separations. Eventually, Ellen bought a butcher's shop of her own on Gladstone Street in Glossop, and Samuel went to work for her.

His father lost his business and lived at a number of temporary addresses but would be allowed to live with Ellen and Samuel occasionally. He seldom stayed with them for long and the last time he had lived with them had been four weeks before the stabbing. He left to move into lodgings in Hulme and earned a little money by working on a casual basis at Water Street abattoir. The last occasion on which he called at Gladstone Street had been on 19 May but his mother would not let him in. Two days later Samuel saw his father who asked him for three shillings as he wished to go to Blackpool where he had been offered a job but Samuel refused.

Ellen was in the habit of travelling to Manchester every Saturday evening and would spend the weekend in the city. She ordered the meat from the abattoir but often mixed business with pleasure. She always returned home on the 5.20pm train, which her husband was aware of.

The inquest into Ellen's death was held before city coroner Mr Gibson on Friday 29 May, at which medical evidence was given which confirmed that her jugular had been severed by a penknife found in the accused's possession. It was at this hearing that Ballington's written account of what had occurred was given:

> I met my deceased wife at London Road Station at two o'clock, and asked how she was and all at home. She made a purchase of clothes in Oldham Street, and I waited outside. She then went to a restaurant in Shudehill, where she had dinner, and I waited outside again for her. We went round the fish market. In the meantime I had asked her for some money. I wanted three shillings for my train fare to go to Blackpool to get work, and she said 'No' I couldn't have it. We got a car at the bottom of Deansgate, and got off again in Water Street near the abattoirs. Afterwards she said she was going to the Ellesmere Hotel to have a drink. I went with her, and she said I would have to pay for my own if I had anything. I said 'I can do'. We went in and we had a bitter each, and we each paid for our own. I begged her again to lend me three shillings and said 'I won't bother you in the market. I will go away'. She said she would not, and in the finish she said she would see me again at London Road Station, and she would see what she could do. I met her at five o'clock at the station. We went on to the platform. I still asked her for this three shillings. We were quiet enough, no disturbance and had no words. She got into the railway carriage, and you know what happened. I did it on the spur of the moment, in mad passion.

There had been three other passengers in the carriage, who provided details of what had occurred immediately before the stabbing and all agreed that Fred Ballington had been sober at

the time. The Ballingtons were standing on the platform and Fred told his wife not to board the train. However, she insisted on doing so, and as she entered the carriage he remained on the platform again asking for money. She refused at first but eventually relented and handed over a handful of change from her purse. However, this did not satisfy Fred who complained 'Eighteen pence is no good'.

He stepped into the carriage and said to his wife: 'Well, I am going and will say goodbye, but we will have a kiss first.' He made an unsuccessful attempt to put his arm around her shoulders, as she resisted him. He continued by saying: 'Well goodbye for ever', and he turned to leave the carriage. Ellen said to him: 'You are a scamp.' Clearly enraged, Fred turned and said: 'I am not.' He stepped back into the train and grabbed her. Moments later there was a scream and Ellen fell to the floor, badly wounded. Her husband held a penknife in his hand and attempted to slash his throat.

Ballington's trial was held at the Manchester Assizes on Tuesday 7 July 1908 before Mr Justice Bucknill. The Crown was represented by Spencer Hogg and the defence was undertaken by Gilbert Jordan. The accused pleaded not guilty to the charges of murder and attempted suicide.

Mr Hogg opened by describing the case as 'a sordid and sad tragedy' which occurred over a trifling amount of money. Details of the deteriorating relationship and the evidence of witnesses on the train were put to the jury. The defence did not deny that their client was responsible for his wife's death, but claimed that the absence of a serious motive meant that he should be convicted of the lesser charge of manslaughter.

However, after having retired for twelve minutes the jury returned to the courtroom with a guilty of murder verdict and the attempted suicide charge was not proceeded with. It was widely reported that when sentencing Ballington to death, the judge was apparently close to tears, which was perhaps because he realised that two people would be dead as a result of such a trivial matter.

Ballington was executed on 28 July at Strangeways Gaol by Henry Pierrepoint and reportedly met his death calmly. At the inquest, held later that day, Dr Edwards stated that the neck wound caused when he cut his own throat had ruptured as he fell through the trap. He had also suffered a fractured skull, which he said was not uncommon when an individual was hanged.

CHAPTER 18

The Burnley Outrage
1909

The nights were drawing in and by 5.30 on the evening of Tuesday 28 December 1909, it was already quite dark as collier William Collins watched his excited three-year-old son John run from the house on Maltkiln Street, Burnley. The little boy was going to meet his mother at the end of the street on her way home from work but fifteen minutes later, when she arrived home she told her husband that she had not seen him. Concerned for his safety, she and her husband contacted the police and a search of the area was made.

Two hours later, twenty-eight-year-old Joseph Wren approached a police sergeant on his beat and said: 'I have done it, I have murdered him.' When asked to explain himself, Wren

Joseph Wren surrenders. Illustrated Police News

continued by saying he had murdered a young boy and had left his body in a field between Bank Hall Colliery and Queen's Park. The sergeant escorted him to the police station and on the way there, Wren said: 'I do not know what made me do it.'

Wren was put in a cell and several officers went to the supposed murder scene. There, just as Wren had said, they found John's body. There was a massive throat wound, so deep that the spinal cord was almost exposed, and lying close to the body were a bloodstained knife and handkerchief.

Later that night, Wren was interviewed by Inspector Jones and made what amounted to a full confession to the crime. He stated that he had seen John earlier at about 5.45pm, and on an impulse picked him up into his arms and carried him to the nearby colliery siding at Bank Hall. There, he strangled him and cut his throat, after which he waited for a few minutes, cut the boy's throat once again and wiped his hands on his handkerchief, which he left at the scene. An hour or so later he decided to surrender to the police and met the sergeant a short time later and advised the officer what he had done.

On the day after the crime had been committed the inquest was held into John's death. Dr Watson confirmed that death had been caused by the injuries arising from the cut throat but the extent of the injuries meant that he could not say one way or the other whether an attempt had been made to strangle him. Later in the day, Wren appeared before the town's magistrates and at both hearings he was committed to stand trial at the next Manchester Assizes. His trial took place on 4 February 1910 before Mr Commissioner Amory, with Gordon Hewart prosecuting and Mr Sandbach defending.

In outlining the Crown's case, Mr Hewart highlighted the unusual features of the crime, namely that a child had been abducted and murdered by a stranger and no motive could be provided as there had been no robbery, nor had there been a sexual assault.

Mr Hewart continued by advising the court that the accused man had served in the Royal Navy for several years as a stoker and had left the service twelve months before committing the crime. He returned to East Lancashire but had been unable to find work and had been on the dole all of that time. On the day of the murder he had walked from Accrington to Burnley where he had met Ernest, his younger brother. Wren told him that he had not eaten for three days and he asked for a cigarette to take the hunger pangs away. He continued by telling Ernest that he would rather go to prison than have to continue to live in poverty without any hope. He was becoming increasingly depressed and felt he was becoming weak minded.

The brothers parted and within minutes Wren came across John Collins. On an impulse he carried the boy away and committed the murder. He had then walked away from the scene and went to Higgins Street in the hope of seeing his own child. Wren was the father of an illegitimate child and adding to his problems was the fact that his former girlfriend, Miss Calvert would not marry him, and he saw little of their child. Later, when interviewed by the police he stated that he might well have murdered his own child had the opportunity arisen before he saw John.

John's body is discovered.
Illustrated Police News

He had continued by telling the police:

I really think I was not in my right senses. I am fully sorry for what I have done, and hope I shall be forgiven by the child's parents. I know the penalty for what I have done and am fully prepared for it.

Wren's barrister, Mr Sandbach, attempted to demonstrate to the jury that his client had been insane at the time he committed the crime. He emphasised the senselessness of the murder, the absence of any rational motive and his immediate surrender and confession to the police. Evidence was produced to show that periodically he suffered from bouts of depression and that in March 1909 he had taken laudanum in a suicide bid after unsuccessfully attempting to persuade Miss Calvert to do the same. He had been heard to threaten to poison himself on more than one occasion. It was also revealed that whilst awaiting his trial he had attempted to hang himself in Strangeways after tying a towel to the ventilator in his cell.

The jury was asked to consider whether at the time of the killing was he aware that what he was doing was wrong. After retiring for fifty minutes the jury decided that he had known and convicted him of wilful murder. He was sentenced to death and taken to the condemned cell at Strangeways.

His solicitor, Mr H Ogden, organised a petition seeking a reprieve for Wren, which considering the nature of the crime, was well supported by the people of Burnley, 2,000 of whom signed it. These were hard times and it seemed that there was some sympathy for this obviously depressed man finding it difficult to deal with unemployment and its consequences. Mr Ogden had also asked the Home Secretary for a special medical investigation to be made. On the Saturday before the scheduled execution the solicitor received a letter from Winston Churchill's private secretary, stating that regrettably, the Home Secretary had been unable to find any grounds justifying a request being made to the King to interfere with the judicial process.

Wren was hanged at Strangeways on Tuesday 22 February 1910 by Henry Pierrepoint, and his assistant John Ellis.

CHAPTER 19

Murdered for the Insurance
1919

It was a little after eight o'clock in the morning of Christmas Eve 1919, a Wednesday, when a man collecting driftwood in the sand hills between St Anne's and Blackpool, and close to the Manchester Convalescent Home, made a horrific discovery. Lying on her back with her left arm across her chest and her right arm over her forehead, was the body of an attractive and fashionably dressed young woman. Later, the police found she had a bank book which confirmed her identity. She was twenty-five-year-old Kathleen Elsie Breaks of Rycroft Farm, Dudley Hill, Bradford, Yorkshire.

Kathleen was found to be still wearing several items of valuable jewellery and no money appeared to have been taken from her pockets. She had removed her wedding ring from her finger and put it in one of her pockets; she had been separated from her husband, John Stoddart Breaks, a Bridlington motor mechanic for eighteen months. Robbery therefore appeared not to have been a motive for the killing.

Enquiries revealed that she had left Bradford the previous day, telling friends she was taking a short break alone in Blackpool. A dinner bill from the previous evening showed that she had booked into the *Palatine Hotel* and after dining, the police were told she had asked a waitress for directions to Lytham.

Dr Arthur Elliott, the district's medical officer, examined the body and initially thought that she had suffered several stab wounds. However, he revised his findings when on the following Sunday, four children playing on the beach close to the crime scene discovered a six-chamber revolver, from which four cartridges had been fired. The body was re-examined and it was discovered that she had died as a result of gunshot

THE VICTIM
MRS BREAKS.

THE BLACKPOOL MYSTERY.

THE ARRESTED MAN
EX-LIEUTENANT F. HOLT.

The body of Kathleen Breaks is discovered in sand hills on the Fylde coast and Holt is arrested. Illustrated Police News

wounds. An inquest was opened at the local police station on 27 December before deputy coroner Harold Parker who took evidence of identification from the deceased's sister, Daisy Muriel Fish of Bradford, before adjourning for the police to complete their enquiries.

Within a matter of hours of her body being discovered, the police had established from her family and letters found in her possessions that for more than a year Kathleen had been having an affair with thirty-one-year-old Frederick Holt. He was a man of independent means and a member of a well known and respectable family from Ansdell near Lytham. He was a former lieutenant in the Loyal North Lancashire Regiment who had been invalided home in mid 1915. In one of the letters Holt referred to her as *My Dear Darling Kathleen.* In another he told her he was lonely without her and described her as *the only being in the world for me.* In one of the most recent he had written *I am sure dear, there will be a day soon when we will never part.*

In the more recent past his letters to Kathleen revealed that he had been pressing her to take out an insurance policy on her life for £10,000, naming him as the beneficiary. Kathleen had no hesitation in agreeing to this but two insurance companies refused to accept the business as they were not married. Nevertheless, Holt had learnt that she could take out such a policy on her own life, and he could receive the money if it was left to him in her will.

Enquiries revealed that a firm of Bradford solicitors had prepared a new will for her, which they had received with her signature in the post on Christmas morning, when she was already dead. Holt and her sister Daisy were named as her executors and he was to receive her wedding ring and £5,000 less £200, which she had insured her own life for.

Holt's bank manager confirmed that his account was overdrawn at the time but this was not a cause for concern as he had sufficient securities in other accounts. Holt was thus not under any immediate financial pressure but the police were satisfied that they had discovered the motive for the crime, as he wanted the cash the insurance policy would provide, and with which they believed he intended travelling abroad.

At the scene of the crime the police had discovered a set of footprints leading away from the body. When they called at Holt's home, a pair of his shoes was seen to be wet and covered with sand. When they were compared with the footprints at the murder scene they were found to be a perfect match. Two bloodstained gloves had also been discovered close to the body and these were similar to a pair Holt was known to have possessed.

The police also interviewed tramcar conductor John Garlick, who had know Holt for many years. He confirmed that at about the time the murder was thought to have occurred, Holt boarded his tram and bought a ticket to a stop close to the Manchester Convalescent Home. Furthermore, John Mills, a tramcar driver reported seeing Holt at a few minutes before 10.30 that night close to where the body was found.

The revolver found near to the murder scene was linked to Holt as its serial number proved it had been bought by the suspect from a Preston gunsmith in August 1914.

At the adjourned inquest, after hearing this evidence, the coroner's jury committed him to stand trial for murder at the Manchester Assizes. However, he still had to appear before the town's magistrates and at that hearing there was an interesting interchange between Holt's solicitor Mr Woosnam, and the deceased's husband John Stoddart Breaks, who had married her in October 1913, after which they had lived together for only five months.

Mr Woosnam demanded to know more about their relationship after the witness had told the court of 'temperamental differences':

Woosnam: Was she bad tempered or were you?
Breaks: No, neither of us. Her point of view did not agree with mine, that was all.
Woosnam: In what way?
Breaks: I can hardly say, we were not suited to each other.
Woosnam: I want to know in what way you disagreed. This is going as a deposition as you know.

At this point, Mr Sims, who was acting as prosecutor stepped in by saying: 'There is no occasion to threaten the witness.'

Breaks: I can only say that my wife was not happy living with me, and she told me so. I don't know whether I ever asked her for a reason.
Woosnam: When did the differences begin?
Breaks: We had differences long before living together. My wife told me she was sorry she was married, as it altered her position in life considerably. I have nothing more definite to tell you.

He confirmed that he had not known of Holt's existence before the murder and that she had returned to live with her mother following their separation. He also stated that she had not sought maintenance from him. Mr Woosnam did not accuse him directly of murdering his wife but the exchange suggested there may be an attempt to imply this at the forthcoming trial. However, her husband impressed as a level headed young man, who was clearly upset by her death, with no feelings of jealousy or any need to rid himself of her in order to avoid paying her regular sums of money, and there would be no further insinuations made.

Nevertheless, there would was to be a dramatic opening on the day the trial was due to start, before Mr Justice Greer, when Holt's barrister, Edward Marshall Hall claimed that his client was insane and should not stand trial. The judge agreed to hear evidence and details were given of his being invalided home from the war in mid-1915 following the bombardment of Festubert. Holt later suffered from chronic rheumatism in his ankle and knees and was in constant pain which had led to his becoming depressed. A medical board in February 1916 had decided he should not return to the front, and he was fit for light duties only.

Dr RP Smith, a former superintendent of Bethlehem Hospital in London, had examined the accused, and he testified that in his opinion Holt was insane and experienced delusions of persecution. Extracts were also read from a letter written by Holt to his solicitor from Strangeways on Christmas Day, in which he described being attacked in the cell by dogs, flies and a swarm of ants. He also wrote that he had been wounded by a mercury-filled bullet.

The prosecution resisted this defence by pointing out that no mention of his supposed insanity had been raised at any earlier hearings, and the jury agreed. It having been established that he was sane and should face trial, a new jury was sworn in.

The trial proper began and the evidence against the accused was overwhelming. An attempt was made to provide an alibi by his parents and sister, but they could not account for his movements at key moments on the night of the murder. In his closing speech, Marshall-Hall claimed the prosecution case was incredible and that a writer of melodramas could not have concocted such a story. However, the jury took less than an hour to convict him of murder and Holt was sentenced to death.

Comments made in Marshall-Hall's closing speech created a storm of protest when he made a scathing attack on 'gloating females who had come to watch a man in peril of his life'. He was criticized from all quarters and in response wrote an open letter a few days later, which read as follows:

> I am afraid my remarks regarding women in court at Manchester Assizes have been misunderstood. They were not directed against nor intended to refer to those women who from legitimate interest either in the case itself or in parties, witnesses, counsel or friends connected with the case were present at the trial I referred to a great crowd of women in the public gallery, numbering as far as I could see at least three hundred.
>
> Anyone who had been obliged, as I was for five days, to pass through this crowd as they came down the stairs would have been quite satisfied from their demeanour and conversation that the words I used correctly described the reason why many of them were there.
>
> Of course women with a legitimate interest have every right to be present, but I only hope that when some day a woman is engaged in defending another woman for her life before a jury of women and a woman judge she will not be handicapped by having to deal with the unpleasant topic of sexual passion in its various forms by a crowd of men in a public gallery, whose object in being there is to satisfy prurient curiosity.

Holt's appeal was heard on 29 March and the defence was allowed to introduce new evidence of heredity insanity on his mother's side. The superintendent of a private lunatic asylum in Essex confirmed that Holt's female cousin was admitted in July 1914 suffering from what was described as 'chronic delusion and insanity with dementia'. An old servant of Richard Rothwell, Holt's maternal grandfather, who used to live in Bury, told of his odd behaviour; he would not drink a cup of tea or coffee without a servant having first tasted it to ensure the drink was not poisoned; and he would not smoke his pipe until someone had first tested the tobacco to ensure it contained no toxic substances.

Holt bids farewell to his distraught parents. Illustrated Police News

Following his return from France, the condemned man had travelled to Malaya where he had contracted syphilis, and it was argued this would have exacerbated his mental health problems. Despite this new evidence the appeal failed.

A heavy rainfall on the morning of his execution in Manchester, did not prevent a large crowd gathering outside Strangeways, as inside, Holt went to his death without posing any problems for executioner John Ellis and his assistant William Willis. However, he maintained his innocence until the end.

The execution. Illustrated Police News

CHAPTER 20

A Misunderstanding that led to Murder
1925

When James Makin and his sweetheart married in early 1925 they could not afford to move into a home of their own immediately and opted to live with his uncle, Joseph Howsley, at 3 Cross Street, Newton Heath, Manchester. They intended staying with him for a few months only, until they could afford to buy a house. In early May, Makin took two days off work and his wife and uncle left him alone in the house when they left for work that morning. At six o'clock that evening they returned home together and she went upstairs to the bedroom she shared with her husband. Within a matter of seconds, Joseph heard a terrific scream and rushed upstairs. There, lying on the bedroom floor, was a body of an unknown young woman.

When Constable Edward Smith arrived he realised that the woman had clearly died in suspicious circumstances and he was soon followed by Superintendent Lansberry. The superintendent made an examination of the almost naked body and noted that most of her clothes were hanging neatly over a chair. She had suffered serious injuries to her throat, and close to the body was a carving knife, covered with blood, together with a broken bottle. Also in the room were a man's coat, shirt and collar, all of which had blood on them, and which were identified as belonging to James Makin. Downstairs, hanging on the scullery door, was a bloodstained towel, which the superintendent believed had been used to wash hands covered with blood. James Makin was nowhere to be seen.

Later, a post-mortem performed by Dr Buck confirmed that the injuries were not self inflicted, nor could they have been caused accidentally. The victim's internal organs were all healthy, and he found a range of external injuries which could only have been the result of a vicious assault, probably with the knife and bottle found with the body. There were three bruises on the back of her head; cuts to both cheeks; and three fingers of her right hand were cut so that the bone was exposed. She had suffered two throat wounds, each of which was caused by a sharp-bladed instrument; the first had penetrated the neck muscle, but the second, a cut five inches in length, had severed the jugular vein, and this had been the cause of death. She was not suffering from a sexual disease.

Two witnesses came forward who provided Superintendent Lansberry with important information. Hilda Collinge, who had a shop opposite 3 Cross Street, saw Makin enter the house alone at 3.30 that afternoon; a few minutes later he appeared at the front door, and after seemingly making sure nobody was watching, he motioned to a young woman, who rushed into the house. Hilda noticed that the woman was wearing a distinctive green hat similar to one found amongst the murdered woman's clothes in Makin's bedroom. An hour later, Hilda saw Makin leave the house alone, and another neighbour, Gertrude Jackson, saw him board a tram on nearby Oldham Road, which was going to Manchester.

Makin spent the next few hours, his last as a free man, in Manchester city centre. He was spotted by a friend, Arthur Green, and the two men made for the *Falstaff Hotel*, where they had several drinks. It was obvious to Arthur that his friend was already drunk, so when he blurted out that he was in trouble because 'I have done a woman in', Arthur, assuming it was the alcohol talking, told him not to be silly and suggested he go home. However, Makin replied: 'I can't go home, its up there I have done it. It was in the wife's bedroom.' Realising he was serious, Arthur initially thought he must have murdered his wife. However, Makin explained that he had picked up a prostitute earlier in the day, and took her home where they had sex. Afterwards, he described an argument taking place, during which he struck her across the head with a bottle, before running downstairs for a knife, with which he returned to the bedroom where he slit her throat.

As he stood up to leave the pub, Makin shook his friend's hand, telling him: 'You are the only pal I have down here

The Falstaff Hotel, *where Makin drank his last pint and confessed to a friend that he had committed a murder.* Manchester Central Library

tonight.' He handed him £9 and asked him to make sure it was given to his wife as he would have no further need for it.

Makin returned by tram to Newton Heath and at 9.45pm walked into the local police station and surrendered to Superintendent Lansberry, who noticed there were recent abrasions on his right hand and his clothing was bloodstained. The suspect was still drunk, and it was not until ten the following morning that he was charged with murder.

The dead woman had by now been identified as twenty-four-year-old prostitute Sara Elizabeth Clutton, also known as Barker and Mary Smith. She was a Liverpudlian but had been living in a woman's hostel on Manor Street in Ardwick.

From Makin's own account of events, taken together with the statements of witnesses, the police were able to produce a picture of what happened on the day of the murder. At noon, Makin was on Market Street, in the centre of Manchester, where he picked up Sara, who agreed to have sex with him. First of all they drank a large amount of alcohol before taking the tram to Newton Heath three hours later.

Once inside 3 Cross Street the couple had sex in the bedroom Makin shared with his wife. Afterwards, she asked for a bowl of water with which she wished to wash her private parts. As she did so she began to cry and when he asked her what was wrong she made no reply. This led him to suspect she had a sexual disease and could have infected him. He became angry, and he told the police that she seemed to become frightened and tried to grab hold of the bottle. However, he managed to get hold of it before she could do so, and as he did she is said to have rushed towards him. Fearing she was about to strike him, he hit her across the head with the bottle.

Although dazed, she began to dress and Makin went downstairs and into the scullery. She shouted: 'Come up here again and I will do you the same as you have done to

Sarah Clutton. Author's collection

me.' Enraged, he took a knife from a drawer and ran back to the bedroom, intending, he later insisted to the police, only to frighten her. However, as he entered the room she rushed at him, and there was a struggle. Both fell to the floor and when Makin stood up he saw blood on his shirt and also streaming from her throat wounds. He claimed he was too drunk to recall everything that happened but he insisted he had not intended to harm her and her death was an accident.

However, the wound which had severed her jugular vein was such that it could not have been caused accidentally, and it was the Crown's case that he had murdered her in a drunken rage, having thought she had possibly infected him with a sexual disease. At the inquest into her death the jury agreed with the latter version of events, as did the magistrates when he appeared before them. Accordingly, he was committed to stand trial at the Manchester Assizes, and on 25 July 1925 he appeared before Mr Justice Wright, Cyril Atkinson MP leading the prosecution and W Gorman the defence.

Makin, who gave evidence on his own behalf and his barrister made no attempt to deny that he was responsible for the killing. The defence was based on insanity, and a good deal

DEAD WOMAN IN CITY HOUSE.

Suspect's Surprise Story to Friend.

BLOW WITH BOTTLE.

'Wilful Murder' Verdict at Inquest.

Makin's account of the crime which he gave to his friend was a major part of the prosecution case at his trial. Author's collection

of evidence was given regarding his background to support this claim.

Makin, whose parents were dead, had served in the Army for three years. Following his discharge, and prior to his marriage, he had lived with his step sister and her husband. They testified that he had suffered from severe headaches and on these occasions he had behaved strangely. It was after he had threatened to kill them both during one of these episodes that he was asked to leave their home. It also emerged that within a few weeks of their marriage, he had threatened his wife with an open razor, but she had been able to take it from him. The members of the jury were also advised of the death of the accused's half brother while an inmate of Prestwich Lunatic Asylum in 1916, where he had been confined for several years.

The jury took twenty minutes to reject his defence strategy and convict him of wilful murder. After being sentenced to death, he was taken to the condemned cell at Strangeways Gaol to await his execution. A petition for a reprieve was signed by 4,000 people, but it could not prevent him being hanged at eight o'clock on the morning of Tuesday 11 August, by William Willis, as a crowd of 250 waited outside the gates.

An inquest was held later that morning, and after it was found that he had died as a result of a judicial hanging, the members of the jury were given a conducted tour of the gaol by the governor.

MYSTERY OF A WOMAN'S DEATH.

Murder Verdict in Newton Heath Tragedy.

The verdict was never really in doubt. Author's collection

CHAPTER 21

The Murder at Nelson 1936

On 22 June 1936, Bracewell Morville walked into Nelson Police Station and informed the officers on duty that a man he described as a dwarf, was selling items of top quality Victorian jewellery in the town's public houses. The seller seemed not to realise just how valuable the items were as he was only asking a pittance for each piece, which led Bracewell to be suspect it was stolen property. Given that Nelson was a small town in East Lancashire, the police believed they knew who it was selling the jewellery. Furthermore, they knew that Ruth Clarkson a seventy-six-year-old spinster, who lived at 56 Clayton Street and who was known to be wealthy despite living in humble circumstances, had such a collection of jewellery. Fearing she had been the victim of a burglary, the police decided to visit her.

Detectives Linekar and Fenton called at the house but there was no response to their repeated knocking. Alerted to the presence of the two officers, concerned neighbours told them that they had not seen Ruth or her beloved dog for several days. The detectives forced open the front door and found the house to be in a filthy state and Ruth had been living in squalor.

A search of the house led to the discovery of Ruth's body in the scullery. She had suffered horrific head injuries and there were bloodstains on the wall and ceiling, which indicated the severity of the assault. A tyre lever smeared with blood was on the floor close to the body. Upstairs, the body of her dog was discovered hanging by its neck from a bedrail. The murderer had gained entry at the rear of the house as the back door showed signs of a forced entry.

Ruth's niece, Mrs Dobney, who lived in nearby Kendal Street, was contacted and she explained that she was aware of

ELDERLY WOMAN FOUND BATTERED TO DEATH IN HER COTTAGE

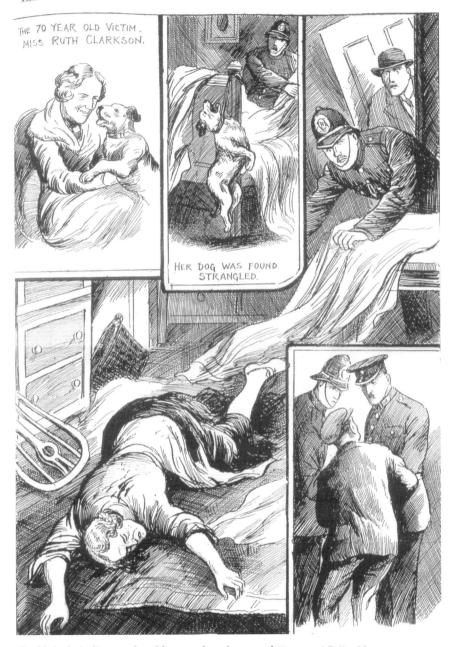

Ruth's body is discovered and her murderer is arrested. Illustrated Police News

the state of her aunt's house, but being a fiercely independent woman, she would not accept any help despite being so frail. She had lived for thirty years with her life-long friend Miss Riley who had died seven years earlier and Ruth had never really recovered. Her niece described her as 'The dearest old woman on earth, who would not hurt a fly.'

The police recognised their chief suspect from the description given by their informant. He was thirty-six-year-old Max Mayer Haslam, who was four feet six inches tall, and was a well-known offender. He was a native of Heywood near Rochdale, and in the past had worked as a cotton spinner. However, in more recent years he had turned to crime and had a number of convictions for burglary. He was known to associate with some of the town's criminals and had recently been released from Strangeways Gaol after completing a one-year sentence for burglary and was known to be living at Routledge's Lodging House.

As they made their way to his lodgings the officers met Haslam, who was with Thomas Barlow, on Pendle Street. Haslam was arrested and later charged with Ruth's murder. His appearance before the local magistrates coincided with the start of Nelson's wakes week, which ensured a packed courtroom, and a crowd of several hundred in the streets surrounding the court building. He was subsequently committed to stand trial at the next Manchester Assizes.

The police were able to build a formidable case against him in the period before the trial. Haslam could not provide an alibi and when arrested he was carrying items of jewellery which he claimed rather unconvincingly were his own. He was found in possession of a key, which he insisted was for a door at his father's house but it was later found not to fit any of his father's doors. However, it did fit the lock of Ruth's back door. It was known that Ruth had put up a fierce struggle and scratches were found on Haslam's body, which he could not explain. There was blood on his shoes and his bloody palm print had been discovered at the murder scene.

The investigators were also provided with significant information by two of Haslam's associates, who lived in the same lodging house as the suspect. Thomas Barlow who was with Haslam at the time of his arrest, and John Davison both claimed that they had seen Haslam knocking on Ruth's door on 19 June. They also said that he had not returned to the lodging house that night. He had eventually got back at a few minutes to eight the following morning in possession of much more cash than he usually had. He was said to have shown them a number of pieces of jewellery, and told them that he had killed a dog during a burglary, although he gave them no further details. Thomas Barlow also stated that Haslam had offered him £200 to help him dispose of a body in a nearby boggy area at Coldwell.

Haslam's trial opened on 8 December 1936 and lasted two days. The judge was Mr Justice Lawrence, the prosecution was led by JC Jackson and the defence by EG Hemmerde. Haslam pleaded not guilty and it was clear from the opening statements that he would be claiming that the Crown's two most important witnesses, Thomas Barlow and John Davison were the true culprits.

From the witness box, Davison testified that on 13 June, he, Barlow and the accused had been in Nelson town centre and walked past Ruth. Barlow had pointed her out and said they should not be misled by her shabby appearance because she was a wealthy woman. A few days later on the nineteenth, the three men were together again but Haslam said he had to go somewhere on his own. The two men followed him and saw him knock on Ruth's front door.

The witness continued by claiming that when Haslam had returned after being out all night he had admitted to him that he had killed Ruth and asked if there were any swamps in the district in which a body could be disposed of. This supported the evidence of Barlow, who had reported being offered money to help Haslam dispose of a body. He denied a defence claim that Bracewell Morville, who was a friend of the witness, had informed on Haslam to the police at the request of Davison and Barlow, as part of a plan to frame him.

Under fierce questioning by Mr Hemmerde, the witness admitted that in the past he had served two prison sentences for shop breaking, and that since the murder had been

George Royle is reprieved but Haslam is executed. Illustrated Police News

committed, he had been charged with stealing from the gas meter at his lodging house.

When Haslam was called into the witness box he told of meeting Davison in Strangeways for the first time earlier in the year when they were both serving prisoners. They arranged for Haslam to go to Nelson when he was released. On his arrival in the town, Haslam and Davison planned a number of 'jobs'. He continued by saying that in early June, he and the other two men had broken into Ruth's house and taken her purse which contained £20.

He further testified that on the night of the nineteenth, the three of them had planned to break into Ruth's home once more. Davison was to leave a window of the lodging house open so they could return late at night without any of the other residents knowing. They were to meet on Clayton Street at midnight, and Haslam testified that despite waiting there for the other two men for some time, they had not turned up and he decided to burgle the property alone.

He made his way to the house and on gaining entry claimed to have discovered Ruth's body. He insisted she was already dead when he arrived at the scene and denied being responsible in the strongest possible terms. He told the court it was his belief that the two others had burgled the property some time earlier without him and were responsible for the murder. However, the jury chose not to believe him and Haslam was convicted and sentenced to death.

Haslam was executed at Strangeways on 4 February 1937. It was to have been a double execution that morning, but George Royle, the man due to stand next to him on the gallows, was reprieved. When Royle had been given the news of his reprieve his first act was to ask his family and friends to pray for Haslam.

CHAPTER 22

A Cheshire Murder
1946

Until the early years of the twentieth century, those convicted of murder in Cheshire had been executed at Chester and later at Knutsford gaols. However, the last hanging at Knutsford took place on 19 March 1912, as during the Great War the gaol was handed over to the Army, and since then the executions of Cheshire's murderers had been carried out in Manchester and Liverpool. This chapter describes one such case.

On the afternoon of Saturday 5 January 1946, fifteen-year-old Frederick Threadgold, a messenger employed by ICI at Winsford, Cheshire was crossing a field close to Smokehall Bridge at Moulton. Part way across, at the bottom of a railway embankment, he discovered the body of a man. The police

Knutsford Gaol. Manchester Central Library

found a bloodstained commando knife underneath the body, and pathologist, Dr WH Grace, confirmed that the dead man had been stabbed once in the back under the left shoulder. He estimated that he had died two days earlier.

The police, led by Superintendent F Platt, chief of Cheshire CID, had little difficulty in identifying the dead man as thirty-seven-year-old Bernard Phillips of Meade Hall Road, Prestwich, near Manchester, who had been employed as a money lender manager by the Refuge Loan Company on Market Street, Manchester. Bernard had been reported missing by his family two days earlier. Superintendent Platt believed the murderer was probably a local man, who knew the isolated spot at which the crime had been committed, ensuring he or she would not be disturbed, and that the body would not be discovered for some time, allowing time for the killer to leave the scene.

At eleven o'clock on the morning of 3 January, a man giving the name George Wood, called at the Refuge Loan Company and applied for a loan of £60. He gave his address as Moss Side Poultry Farm, Tarporley in Cheshire, which he offered as a security against the loan. Bernard agreed to drive the man to the farm in the company car, and he took £50 in cash, which included two five pound notes. The two men left the building together and Bernard was never seen alive again.

The police were given a description of the man who applied for the loan, and it was not long before they focused on a thirty-year-old local man, Harold Berry of Ledward Street, Wharton. He was a nightwatchman, employed at the local Co-operative Wholesale Society bacon factory, earning £5 weekly with which to keep his wife Jessie and their four children. Nevertheless, he was in London that weekend with another young woman, and there were indications that he must have come into possession of a considerable amount of money in the recent past. The police awaited his return and he was arrested at a house on Seedley Road, Salford and at two o'clock the following morning he was charged with Bernard's murder to which he replied: 'Not guilty.'

There was no forensic evidence linking the suspect to the crime, nor were there any eyewitnesses. However, there was a great deal of circumstantial evidence. A search of his house led to the discovery of a bloodstained coat and £22. 10s. in cash. Furthermore, he was known to have possessed a knife, which he bought in December 1945 from workmate Charles Bratt for ten shillings, which was similar to that used in the murder, and which he was now unable to produce.

The police also learnt that he had bought a new coat for five guineas from tailor William Dodd on Winsford High Street, which was another indication that he had cash to spend. A witness confirmed that Berry had arrived at the CWS farm in Shropshire several hours after the murder and bought some eggs, and he was in a car similar to that of the victim. When the car was discovered later on Moulton Hall Lane on 4 January, eggs were found on the back seat, and police were convinced Berry had driven the car after killing his victim.

Following his arrest, he was searched and he was found to have a wallet and cigarette lighter, which were later confirmed to have belonged to Bernard. Also, a colleague of the deceased identified Berry as the man who visited the office giving the name George Wood.

Another damning revelation was the fact that Berry had spent the weekend after the murder in London with twenty-one-year-old Irene Wynn, the wife of a soldier serving overseas. The police believed this provided the motive for the

He Found Dead Moneylender
"DEATH TOOK PLACE 2 DAYS BEFORE"
By A STAFF REPORTER

The discovery of the victim's body is reported. Author's collection crime, as he needed to raise money to afford the weekend away. On 5 January, the couple travelled first class by train to London Euston, and stayed in a hotel for two nights. He registered in his own name and gave his correct address, but the receptionist Gladys Ramsay provided confirmation by identifying him and Irene. He paid the bill in five pound notes, and these were later found to have been those issued to Bernard when he left the office for the last time.

Irene was an innocent party and she co-operated fully with the police. She revealed that he had much more cash than his wages alone could have provided him with; he took her to the cinema, the theatre, bought her flowers, treated her to expensive meals, bought her two books, and paid seventeen shillings and sixpence for a bunch of grapes, which were still a great luxury in post-war England. She also had her purse stolen and he offered to replace the cash she had lost but Irene refused his offer.

Berry's trial was held in Chester before Mr Justice Stable between 11 and 14 February 1946. Glyn Jones prosecuted and Edmund Davies defended the accused. There was a dramatic scene in court early in the trial as Dr Grace re-enacted the crime with a volunteer policeman by grabbing him from behind, and demonstrating the angle at which the knife had entered the body of the deceased.

The defence attempted to prove that Berry had come into possession of the cash he had by means other than the murder. A friend, Kelvin Allcock testified that on 18 December 1945, he gave Berry £11. 5s. for nine pullets (young hens). Berry also swore that on 3 January he had received £17. 1s. 6d. from a street bookie named George, which were the winnings from a bet he had placed two months earlier. He claimed to have staked seven shillings on an outsider at odds of 40 to 1, but under cross-examination he failed to name the horse or the date of the race.

When he gave his evidence, Berry also told of a meeting he had with a sailor he knew from his merchant navy days, named William Greenwood, on 3 January. His old friend had been driving a car, which he claimed must have been the victim's, and drove Berry to the farm in Shropshire where he had bought the eggs. Berry also claimed that it was his former shipmate who had given him the wallet and cigarette lighter.

In his summing up the judge warned the jury not to be influenced by the accused's immoral behaviour with Irene, and that they should base their decision on the evidence alone. He pointed to the failure of the defence to provide any proof of the existence of William Greenwood and the absence of any proof regarding the bet he had supposedly made. The summing up took over three hours, but it took the jury just forty-five minutes to convict Berry of murder.

A murder committed during a robbery meant there was little hope of a reprieve, and Berry was hanged at Strangeways on 9 April 1946 by Thomas Pierrepoint.

CHAPTER 23

A Miscarriage of Justice
1949

I t was shortly after nine o'clock on the night of Saturday 19 March 1949, when a number of shots were heard coming from the office of the manger of the Cameo Cinema in Wavertree, Liverpool. Patrick Griffin, a member of the cinema staff, ran to the office and was confronted by a masked man brandishing a pistol. He threatened to shoot Patrick if he came any closer, before rushing out into the street and disappearing into the night.

Inside the manager's office there were signs of a desperate struggle, and lying on the floor was the thirty-nine-year-old manager, Leonard Thomas of Melwood Drive, West Derby, and slumped in a chair was the twenty-five-year-old assistant manager, John Bernard Catterall, and both had been shot.

The gunman had cut the cinema's telephone line, but an ambulance eventually arrived to take the pair to Smithdown Road Hospital. Leonard had been shot once, through the left side of his chest and was dead on arrival. John had been shot three times and it was a wound to the back which proved to be the fatal bullet for he died a little later without having regained consciousness.

This was clearly a robbery that had gone wrong as the night's takings of just over £50 were still in the bag in which cashier Nellie Jackson had carried them to the office a few minutes before the shootings. It appeared that the two friends had refused to hand over the money and resisted the gunman, who had shot them, panicked and fled the scene empty handed. Tests would later reveal that the murder weapon was probably a self-loading German P 38 pistol, although it was never found.

The police believed that the killer must have known the layout of the building and the staff routine, and had waited until he knew the cashier would have taken the cash to the office. Although of limited value, Patrick was able to provide some details of the gunman. He was five feet eight inches tall, of medium build and had dark hair. He was wearing a brown double-breasted and belted tweed coat, black shoes and a trilby turned down at the front. The police told the press they were confident of an early arrest, but in fact they had little to go on, and despite interviewing hundreds of Liverpool's known criminals, no progress was made in the early stages of the investigation.

However, on 4 April, the police received an anonymous letter, which opened with the writer insisting he was not a crank and that its contents were genuine. The writer indicated he knew the two men who were responsible for the shootings, but he did not name them. One had lost his nerve when they arrived at the Cameo and had remained outside and did not participate in the shootings. The letter writer wanted assurances that if he came forward, revealed his identity and testified for the Crown, that he would not be prosecuted. He confirmed that he had a criminal record and that he had been present when the crime was planned but did not want to become involved. The letter continued by claiming the murder weapon had been thrown into a lake in the park in Edge Lane, but it was never found despite an extensive search and the use of a magnet and mechanical grab.

The letter ended with a request that the police insert a message in the personal column of a local newspaper confirming the terms insisted upon were acceptable and the writer would not be prosecuted. This they did, but weeks passed and nothing more was heard from the letter writer. That was until late September when James Northam came forward. He was a petty criminal who also acted as pimp for his girlfriend, prostitute Jaqueline Dickson, who also claimed to have been present when the crime was planned.

The couple named twenty-seven-year-old George Kelly and twenty-six-year-old Charles Connolly as being those responsible. When they were arrested, Kelly denied knowing his alleged partner insisting: 'I have never seen him in my life.'

George Kelly. Author's collection

Connolly said: 'I have never been in the Cameo Cinema in my life.'

However, Northam and Dickson told a different story. They claimed to have been with the two suspects at eight o'clock on the night of the murders, in the *Bee Hive* pub on Mount Street, and Kelly was accompanied by a young woman whose identity they did not know. The group of five began discussing burglaries they might commit, and Connolly mentioned the Cameo Cinema. He told them they would have to wait until after nine o'clock, when the cashier took the takings to the manager and it would have to be 'a stick-up job'.

Kelly was said to have been keen on the suggestion and pulled a pistol and some bullets from his pocket and loaded it. He said he needed a mask, and after finding his own handkerchief was too small, the young woman handed him an apron, which she took from her handbag. He asked Northam for his overcoat as it was cold. Kelly and Connolly decided they would take a tram and left with Dickson, Northam having got cold feet on seeing the gun. After a few minutes, Dickson returned to the pub as she too had become worried that Kelly was armed.

Northam and Dickson claimed that on the following day, they were in the *Bee Hive* and met Connolly who was with James Skelly, and Kelly, who was with the same young woman as on the previous evening. Connolly appeared to be on edge and said he planned to leave the country, to which Kelly responded by calling him a 'yellow bastard'. He told Connolly to deny knowing him if he was questioned by the police. Connolly said he would and added that he had set up an alibi with his wife. Kelly turned to Northam and Dickson, making it clear that they would be killed should they tell the police anything.

The following day, Kelly returned the overcoat to Northam and told him why the job went wrong. He blamed Connolly for losing his nerve when they arrived, and not keeping watch properly. Kelly was in the office pointing his gun at the manager, and was taken by surprise when his assistant walked in, and told Kelly: 'Put that toy away.' He began to struggle with Kelly who continued by telling Northam: 'I couldn't be bothered with him anymore', and so, according to Northam, he began shooting.

In the days leading to the trial Kelly and Connolly were held on remand in Walton Gaol, but were kept apart so they could not communicate directly with each other. One of their fellow inmates, Robert Graham, who was serving a sentence for obtaining money by false pretences, approached the police with what he described as important information. He claimed to have exercised regularly with each of the accused on alternate days, and in a statement to the police he said that Connolly had told him he was waiting outside the cinema and had not taken part in the shootings. He also said that Kelly had told him: 'I shot both men.'

The police had realised the significance of proving that Kelly and Connolly had known each other for some time, despite their claims not to have met prior to their arrests. The police insisted they had met during the Second World War at Tor Point, a Royal Navy training establishment. Detective Sergeant Richardson of the Liverpool police and James Sangster, a store manager who claimed to know the two accused, came forward to testify that the two men did know each other very well.

The trial opened in mid-January 1950, and the Crown's main witnesses were Northam, Dickson and Graham. The defence claimed that the first two mentioned witnesses may well have been present when the crime was planned, but their fellow conspirators had not been Kelly and Connolly. In agreeing to testify against them, they were attempting to ensure the real culprits were not caught and at the same time, save their own skins.

Charles Connolly.
Author's collection

The defence poured scorn on their evidence, suggesting it was ridiculous to suggest that in a pub on a busy Saturday night, a plan to commit the robbery was finalised, a gun and ammunition was produced, and a handkerchief tied around Kelly's face to see if it would be suitable for a mask.

Nevertheless, Northam created a sensation when giving his evidence as he said he had been approached by Kelly's solicitor and offered a bribe of £150 not to testify at the trial. Furthermore, Kelly had signed a statement implicating Northam much more deeply in the crime than he was admitting to, which would be handed to the police if he did not agree not to testify or to change his evidence. However, Northam stated he had decided that he would not be intimidated nor would he accept a bribe. This claim was of course rejected out of hand by the defence.

As for Graham's evidence, the defence described him as a wholly unscrupulous and unreliable character, motivated by a desire to gain early release from his sentence. He also confirmed that he had in the past spent some time in a mental hospital.

Both of the accused provided alibis for the night of the murders. James Skelly testified that he had been with his friend Kelly that night at the *Leigh Arms*. He acknowledged that Kelly had left him for a brief time at about 9.15, saying he was going for a drink at another nearby pub, but he was back within half an hour. This was backed up by Frederick Tomalla, the landlord of the *Leigh Arms*. A customer, James Currie, remembered that Kelly was certainly in the pub at 9.50, as he offered to buy drinks for a number of customers.

Connolly's mother testified that her son had spent the early part of the Saturday evening at her house. His wife and sisters testified that he had arrived at a dance at St Mark's Church

Hall, where he entered a rumba competition. Two young women, Teresa McCormack and Elizabeth Dickson supported this evidence. However, Charles McVane, the organiser of the dance stated that he had not seen Connolly until ten o'clock, and remembered this clearly as the accused man had kept his trilby on as he danced.

In his summing up the judge advised the jury that they would have to consider whether the evidence given by the Crown's three main witnesses could be relied on. He also mentioned the alibi evidence and raised the possibility that Kelly and Connolly may have drawn attention to themselves deliberately, after committing the crime, one by offering to buy a large number of drinks and the other by wearing his hat at the dance, as this might help them with their alibis.

The jury was unable to reach a verdict and a second trial was ordered, which began on 2 February and lasted for six days. However, the Crown opted for a new strategy, and offered Connolly the opportunity of saving himself from a possible death sentence. On legal advice he accepted the proposal that he plead guilty to conspiracy to rob. Kelly thus appeared alone in the dock to face the murder charge, and although Connolly did not give evidence against him, his case was clearly undermined. He was found guilty and sentenced to death. Connolly was subsequently sentenced to ten years' imprisonment.

Kelly appealed but this failed as the Home Secretary found no grounds to grant a reprieve. Kelly was executed on Tuesday 28 March 1950 at Walton Gaol by Albert Pierrepoint, who was assisted by Syd Dernley. Connolly died in 1997 protesting his innocence to the end.

There were many who believed both men to have been innocent given that they were convicted despite the absence of a weapon, a lack of forensic evidence and no eyewitnesses. Eventually, in February 2001, the Court of Appeal agreed to reconsider the case. The Liverpool police had allowed supporters of the two men access to their files, and among the documents they found a statement made in September 1949 by Robert Graham, saying a prisoner named Donald Johnson had admitted committing the crime.

Walton Gaol. Liverpool Central Library

The Crown accepted the document was genuine and that the defence had not been told of its existence at the time. The convictions of both men were quashed on 10 June 2003, despite the Crown's opposition to Connolly's being dealt with in this manner. At the hearing, Lord Justice Rix said: 'However much the Cameo murders remain a mystery, we regard the circumstances of Kelly and Connolly's trials as a miscarriage of justice which must be deeply regretted.'

The police have said that there will be no further investigation into the crime itself or the actions of the senior detectives involved at the time. Nevertheless, there are still those seeking a public inquiry, and we may not yet have heard the last of this case.

CHAPTER 24

The Death of a Nightwatchman
1952

On Sunday 12 August 1952, the badly beaten body of fifty-eight-year-old George Camp, a one-eyed nightwatchman, was found in his hut on the Crossacres estate, Wythenshawe, Manchester. Thefts of valuable materials from the many building sites in the area were rife and many thousands of pounds worth had been stolen. However, nothing of significance seemed to be missing, and the police thought it unusual that the killer or killers, who had not been disturbed, should leave the site empty handed. A motive other than theft therefore seemed likely.

George was a single man, whose only companion was his dog Peggy, later found cowering in a nearby farm building. He had no settled address and for the previous few years had been living in local hostels. One of his brothers described him as a quiet and inoffensive man, and the family could not think of anybody who held a grudge against him.

Pathologist Dr GB Manning performed a post-mortem and catalogued the injuries sustained by the deceased. He suffered nineteen fractures to his ribs, an arm was broken, his head was badly bruised and his liver had been ruptured. The injuries had been caused by an axe and plank which were lying close to the body and which were covered in blood. There was evidence of a fierce struggle and buttons had been torn from his coat and trousers.

On one of the outside walls of the hut there were blood smears, and a strand of the victim's hair was also discovered. The police formed the view that he had been in the open when assaulted with the axe and as he attempted to seek refuge in his hut, he had leaned against the outside wall, leaving the blood and hair as he did so. However, he did not find safety

Crossacres. Manchester Central Library

and the assault continued when he was inside the hut. The charred remains of George's identity card and ration book were discovered on the brazier.

A team of forty detectives were assigned to the case and a murder headquarters was set up at Moor End Police Station in Wythenshawe, under Detective Chief Superintendent Dan Timpany, head of the Manchester Criminal Investigation Department. The team appeared to have made an early breakthrough and within the first two days issued descriptions of two men they wished to trace. One had been seen playing cards with George in the *Red Lion Hotel* in Gatley on the Friday night before he died. He was described as being five feet six inches tall, with a fresh complexion, good clean teeth, and was wearing a brown striped suit. The other man of interest was a thin-faced Irishman with dark hair and wearing a black overcoat, who was seen boarding the all night bus to Manchester at Crossacres in the early hours of Sunday morning.

However, there was to be no immediate breakthrough in the case, as neither of the men could be identified or traced. Three weeks later, the crime was believed to have been linked to the murder of a widow in Liverpool and the subsequent suicide of the alleged perpetrator who had ties with Manchester. However, this proved not to be so and the police were no further forward.

In the two months following the murder, the police had visited almost 6,000 homes and checked on the movements of 600 individuals. However, Detective Timpany and his team had made little headway, although the situation changed dramatically when Gilbert Hair, the governor of Strangeways, made contact.

On 8 November, a prisoner, twenty-four-year-old Alfred Bradley of Macclesfield, who was in the gaol on other matters, had asked for a meeting with Mr Hair, at which the prisoner admitted that he had been present at the time of the nightwatchman's death, and claimed that the murder had been committed by two companions he would not name. When later seen by the police he volunteered to return to the scene of the crime and was driven around the area. He convinced Detective Timpany that he knew a great deal about the crime as he pointed out a number of sewer shafts which Bradley rightly suggested were not there on 12 August, as they had indeed been constructed after that date.

On 12 November, Bradley was again interviewed by the police, and on this occasion he stated that only one other man had been present when the murder was committed. Later the same day, he changed his story once again, which police believed was closer to the truth. He admitted that he had killed the night watchman with several blows of the axe found at the scene, and he had acted alone. He told his interviewer: 'I don't want my father to know the type of life I have been leading. I have been indecent with Camp regularly for which he paid me. That night he gave me beer, about ten pints. I am not used to beer. I was so disgusted with myself I killed him with the axe. I have been doing this for many years, since I was taught by a rich man who paid me.' At the conclusion of his statement he confirmed he had stolen £16 from the deceased and added: 'I had no intention of killing him. The money and drink did it.'

It had been eighty-six days since the crime was committed, when on 6 November Bradley appeared before the city's stipendiary magistrate, Mr FB Turner. Detective Chief Inspector Harold Green advised him of the interviews with Bradley but gave no further details, and asked that he be remanded in custody for seven days. He confirmed that on that occasion a representative of the Director of Public Prosecutions would be present. However, Mr Turner refused to comply with this request on the basis of the information he had been provided with. He said to the police officer: 'What is there to associate this man with Camp's death? You have told me nothing yet to justify this remand.'

Chief Inspector Green replied: 'This man has made a statement', but had to acknowledge, when Mr Turner persisted, that he did not have a copy with him in court.

Mr Turner commented: 'I think I should see the statement before I remand this man', and turning to the accused, told him: 'You will be stood down until this statement is produced in court.'

Forty-five minutes later the signed statement was handed to Mr Turner, who after reading it advised Bradley: 'I have read part of the statement and on that of course you will have to be remanded.'

Bradley's trial opened on 29 November at the Manchester Assizes before Mr Justice Lynskey. The defence called Bradley to give evidence. In the witness box he stood with one hand in his pocket as he took the oath. His barrister, Kenneth Burke's first question was: 'Is your name Alfred Bradley?' to which the prisoner simply nodded his head. The judge asked him: 'Well is it?' and when Bradley replied it was, the judge said: 'Well say so. It is very important from your point of view that those gentlemen on the back row of the jury should hear everything you say. So will you speak up so that they can do so?'

The Court demanded to see relevant documents. Author's collection

Confessed in gaol to hut murder, court told

"PREYED ON MIND"

At his trial the jury was told that Bradley confessed to the murder whilst in gaol on other matters. Author's collection

A shocked courtroom watched as the accused picked up the bible and threw it at the judge, shouting: 'I've finished.' A glass of water at the judge's side was knocked over and Bradley was restrained by the dock officers and taken down into the cells, struggling fiercely. The judge asked Dr Cormack, the medical officer at Strangeways Gaol, who was at court as a witness, to examine Bradley. The doctor later reported that Bradley was in a highly overwrought state and was not in a fit condition to give evidence. The judge expressed his concern that the jury members might not be able to put what they had seen out of their minds, which could be prejudicial to the accused. He therefore directed that he should appear before another jury at a later date, stating: 'I am acting in unprecedented conditions and have no precedent to work on.'

The following week, Bradley appeared before a new jury and trial judge, Mr Justice Stable. His barrister, Mr Burke, addressed the jury and proposed a dual defence. He argued that firstly, the death was an accident and highlighted part of the evidence that had been presented earlier in the trial by prosecution witness Dr Manning, who had testified that the initial injuries sustained by the victim were probably not fatal. Furthermore, in replying to a question posed by the judge, Dr Manning had conceded that the fatal injuries could have

Bible is hurled at murder-trial judge

The first trial was abandoned after the accused threw a Bible at the judge. Author's Collection

been caused by the plank falling on him. Mr Burke argued that it was possible therefore, that his client had assaulted the deceased, but these injuries did not kill him. George had then struggled into the hut, seeking refuge, but the plank had toppled over on to him, causing his death. Later, a third unknown person had entered the hut, lifted the plank away from the body, and fled in a panic without reporting the discovery of the body.

Not satisfied with this ingenious theory, Mr Burke proposed a second possible explanation, by claiming that his client might have killed him, but was provoked into doing so. If he could persuade the jury that this was so, Bradley would be convicted of the lesser charge of manslaughter. He claimed that George was a homosexual who had been paying Bradley over a long period of time for sexual favours. On the night of his death he had paid the young man money and also provided a great deal of alcohol. Perhaps Bradley had said he had become disgusted with their relationship and no longer wished to indulge in such behaviour. The older man had possibly threatened to inform his parents of what he had been doing if he refused to continue to see him. In such circumstances, Bradley should be convicted of manslaughter.

After retiring for fifty minutes, the jury rejected both hypothetical scenarios and convicted Bradley of murder. He was hanged at Strangeways Gaol on Tuesday 15 January 1952.

CHAPTER 25

The Murder of Auntie Bella
1962

It was Friday 4 May 1962, and David Cross and his wife Sarah Isabella were living in Miles Platting, Manchester, having moved from Burnley several years earlier. However, they retained strong links with the Lancashire cotton town, and were looking forward to travelling to Wembley the next day to watch their home town team play Tottenham Hotspur in the FA cup final. David left home to go to work at the Royal Ordinance Factory in Patricroft, leaving his fifty-eight-year-old wife, known affectionately as 'Auntie Bella' in charge of the small newsagents and tobacconist shop they owned on Hulme Hall Lane. Sadly, the couple would not make the journey south.

Later that day, at 4.50pm, nine-year-old Stephanie Howarth entered the shop, intending to buy a bar of chocolate. Nobody came to serve her and she peered over the counter, behind which she saw Auntie Bella lying on the floor. Thinking she had fainted, Stephanie ran for her sister, Doreen Kenyon, who came and was shocked to discover that the shopkeeper was dead, and had been the victim of a severe beating.

The police were able to establish with some accuracy the time of her death, as a wholesale tobacconist had dropped off a delivery at 4.25pm, and he confirmed the shopkeeper had been in good spirits. Her murderer had therefore struck in the twenty-five minutes before Stephanie arrived.

Three shillings remained in the till which had been forced open, and nine shillings was discovered under the body. The drawers in a desk in the back room had also been forced open, and robbery had been the motive, for after a distraught David had been advised of his wife's death, he confirmed that the week's takings of almost £80 would have been in the till.

Surrounding the body on the floor of the shop was the glass and contents of five shattered pop bottles, which had been used to attack the victim. She had put up a spirited defence as

Hulme Hall Lane. Manchester Central Library

there were bruises and scratches to her arms, and some hair had been pulled out by the roots. A post-mortem later confirmed that death had resulted from a fractured skull.

The door to the yard at the rear of the shop was always kept locked, but was now open, and this was the escape route taken by the killer. A search for fingerprints in that part of the premises proved to be successful, for the full print of the middle finger of a left hand was found on the scullery door, together with two partial prints.

The police reviewed the papers of two earlier crimes which remained unsolved, as there were similarities. In August 1957, sixty-five-year-old Alice Moran had been beaten and stabbed to death in her Manchester sweetshop. Also in 1957, eighty-year-old Emily Pye had been battered to death in her Halifax corner shop. However, the detectives leading the inquiry could find no links and became convinced that it was a local man who was responsible for Auntie Bella's murder. A good deal of progress was in fact being made, which Detective Inspector Tony Fletcher, a fingerprint expert with the Manchester police, gave details of in his memoirs *Memories of Murder,* which was published some years later.

In the early 1960s it was not always possible to make an immediate match with the prints found at the scene of a crime and those already on record, and this was so in this case. Nevertheless, the prints from the murder scene were used initially to clear a man who made a false confession. He had been discovered in the yard of Auntie Bella's shop a few days after the murder. He was detained and as he was being questioned, it emerged he knew details of the crime and the interior of the shop that had not been published. However, when his prints were compared to those from the scullery door, they did not match. This did not prove the man was innocent, but he was released on the orders of the lead detective, despite the objections of some of his colleagues. He had a hunch he was not their man and continued with his house to house enquiries and also taking fingerprints voluntarily from the men in the district.

Three weeks after the murder the prints from the shop were matched with a set already held on police files, those of twenty-six-year-old James Smith. He was arrested at his home on Corfe Street, on the morning of Sunday 27 May.

Smith worked as a rubber moulder for Ferguson Shiers Ltd in Failsworth, and a check with the firm showed that he had finished the day shift at noon on the day of the murder. When questioned about his movements that afternoon, he said he had first of all had a haircut, and later met three of his workmates at the *Sun Inn*. His friends left him between 2.30 and 3.00, after which he insisted he went home. He acknowledged that he passed the shop in which the murder was committed but insisted that he did not go in and knew nothing of the murder.

As an alibi, he told police that his insurance agent had called at his home that afternoon at 4.30, and if this was so, he could not have committed the murder in the time available. However, the agent, John Hamilton, could not remember if he saw Smith or not, but he was adamant that he would not have called at the house before 4.45. A walk between the shop and Smith's house confirmed it could be done in a time that would have allowed him to have committed the murder and walk home before the insurance agent had called.

Smith was charged with the murder to which he replied: 'You don't expect me to say anything do you?' Tony Fletcher notes that at this point, a confident Smith bet a detective £5 that he would not hang. The police realised there was a significant weakness in their case, because despite his fingerprints being found on the scullery door, which proved Smith had been on the premises in the immediate past, this alone did not place him at the scene when the murder was

Corfe Street. Manchester Central Library

committed. Nevertheless, the painstaking work of Detective Chief Inspector Louis Allen at the North Western Forensic Science Laboratory in Preston would prove to be conclusive.

Following his arrest, a thorough search had been made of Smith's home. Using a vacuum cleaner to gather up any fibres and other trace evidence, a small fragment of glass was sucked up from down the side of the cushions on his settee. This was taken to the laboratory at Preston, where Chief Inspector Allen had previously been given the shattered remains of the five broken bottles used to commit the murder. With great skill, patience and a tube of glue, he had reconstructed all five bottles. When handed the piece found at Smith's home it was found to fit perfectly into a gap where a fragment was missing. The police now had proof that Smith had been present when the murder took place.

Smith's trial took place at Liverpool Assizes between 15 and 18 October 1962, before Mr Justice Stable. Glynn Burrell led for the Crown and Godfrey Hellpern represented the accused. At the conclusion of the trial the jury took just twenty minutes to convict him of capital murder and he was executed six weeks later, at Strangeways, on 28 November, thus becoming the last person to be executed for a murder committed in Lancashire.

CHAPTER 26

The Final Act
1964

History was made on the morning of Thursday 13 August 1964, when a pair of inept thugs, twenty-four-year-old Gwynne Owen Evans and twenty-one-year-old Peter Anthony Allen, were executed simultaneously in Liverpool and Manchester, thus becoming the last two to hang in the United Kingdom.

In the early hours of Tuesday 7 April that year, Joseph Fawcett heard loud noises, followed by screams, coming from the house of his next door neighbour, bachelor John Alan West, at 28 King's Avenue, Seaton, near Workington, Cumberland. Concerned for his neighbour's welfare, Joseph went to the house, but there was no response when he knocked on both the front and back doors. He had however, noticed a car unknown to him, driving away from the scene at high speed. He alerted the police, and on gaining entry to number 28, they discovered John's body; and close to the body, also found a cosh with which he had been beaten. He had sustained twelve serious head injuries and had also been stabbed in the chest.

John had recently received two inheritances, the first of which he received following the death of his mother, and the second came after the suicide of a sister. Robbery was thought to be the most likely motive, and following a search of the house, a watch and two bankbooks were found to be missing. A raincoat which the police knew did not belong to the dead man, for in one of the pockets they found a medallion bearing the name G O Evans, had been left at the scene. Another item which proved to be of great significance to the investigation was a piece of note paper bearing the name of Norma O'Brien. She was quickly traced and found to be a seventeen-year-old Liverpool factory worker, who informed the police that the medallion belonged to Gwynne Owen Evans, whose real name was John Robson Welby. She had met him the previous year when visiting her sister in Preston, and she was able to confirm that she had seen

Evans wearing the medallion and also to provide his address.

Evans was arrested and under questioning incriminated Allen, with whom he lodged on Clarendon Street, Preston. When Allen was detained, police found that he was in possession of the murdered man's watch. The two dairymen had little alternative other than to admit having been involved in the crime. Evans had worked with John, a van driver for a local laundry in the past, and had decided to visit him in the hope of borrowing money. Allen, his wife and two children, accompanied him on the drive to Seaton in a stolen car. However, as they had called at the house on King's Avenue in the early hours of the morning, it was difficult to claim that it was a friendly social visit. When

Peter Anthony Allen. Author's collection

charged with the murder, Owens replied: 'I want to apologise for all the inconvenience I have caused and I am very sorry.' Allen said: 'I am very sorry for all I have done.'

Further questioning of the suspects revealed that it had been Evans who had suggested the trip to Cumberland, and he admitted stealing John's watch. An argument had followed John's refusal to give a loan, and at this point, the accounts of the two men differed. Each claimed to have taken no part in the beating and stabbing of the victim, and insisted that the other man had been the murderer.

Their trial opened on 1 July 1964 before Mister Justice Ashworth at the Manchester Assizes. The antagonism each of the defendant's bore against the other was evident, and they had to be kept apart in the dock. Clearly, each was attempting to save his own life at the expense of the other. The decision as to whether a murderer would hang was now determined by the provisions of the Homicide Act 1957, which restricted the use of the death penalty. In certain circumstances the charge could be reduced from murder to that of voluntary manslaughter, as the notion of diminished responsibility was introduced, and also in cases of failed suicide pacts, when one of the parties survived.

Allen's wife Mary was called as a witness on his behalf in an attempt to support his claim that although he acknowledged taking part to a limited extent, Evans had been responsible for much of the beating. He was also adamant that Evans had used the knife as he said: 'Jack would recognise me.' From the dock, Mary described the bitter hatred she now felt for Evans, and an extract from one of her letters to him, sent as the pair awaited their trial on remand read:

> How could you lie after knowing that Peter is taking all the blame and will probably hang for murder.

Gwynne Owen Evans. Author's collection

However, she had to concede that she could provide no proof that her husband was not involved in the killing.

Of significance in the trial of Owen and Evans, was the abolition of constructive malice. Prior to the Act anyone convicted of killing a victim as another felony was being committed, was guilty of murder, even if the death was caused accidentally. After 1957, this was no longer so, and the prosecution had to prove that the accused had intended to kill or seriously injure the victim.

Evans and Allen were charged with the offence of capital murder, introduced by the Act, and which applied firstly in instances of theft, secondly by shooting or by causing an explosion, thirdly when resisting arrest, fourthly killing an on duty police officer and finally killing an on duty prison officer. The death penalty was also retained for repeated murders, which was when an individual was convicted of two killings committed on two separate occasions in the United Kingdom.

As the trial progressed, Mr Justice Ashworth required the jury to consider a key point; they had to decide if the murder had been committed by one of the two men, or by one of them acting alone, for if they decided it was the latter scenario he would be guilty of capital murder and hang, but the other would be convicted of non capital murder, and would thus not face execution. The jury found both men to be equally guilty of capital murder, and in the final act of the trial, which closed on 7 July, the judge sentenced both men to death.

The hangman Harry Allen always wore a bow tie when he carried out an execution.
Author's collection

Others would afterwards be convicted of capital murder and sentenced to death, but all were later reprieved, and the last of these was David Chapman at Leeds on 1 November 1965. The death penalty for murder was suspended for five years, and was finally abolished in December 1969. This had been a lengthy process, which began to make headway in the first half of the nineteenth century. It was during this period that the last hangings took place of forgers, coiners, burglars, arsonists, rapists and thieves, together with those convicted of sacrilege, stealing letters, and returning from transportation. Thus, by 1861, only murder, with one or two exceptions in war time, remained a capital crime. Also during this period, the rules governing insanity were tightened, and the execution of juveniles was outlawed.

There had been those who had argued that women should not be executed under any circumstances, and although this argument did not prevail, there were limited gains in the early twentieth century, when infanticide became a non-capital offence.

Owen was hanged by Harry Allen at Strangeways and Allen was hanged at Walton by Robert Stewart, unaware that they were making history of a kind.

Strangeways Gaol. Manchester Central Library

Sources and Bibliography

Fletcher, Tony, *Memories of Murder,* Weidenfield and Nicholson, 1986

Jackson, Valentine, *Remarkable Trials at the Lancaster Assizes, Held 1806 at Lancaster before Sir Robert Graham, Knight.* R Butters, 1806

Taylor, George, *A Correct Report of the Trial of William Holden, James Ashcroft the Elder, James Ashcroft the Younger, David Ashcroft and John Robinson,* J Pratt, 1817

Newspapers
Burnley Gazette
Illustrated Police News
Liverpool Daily Post
Liverpool Echo
Liverpool Mercury
Manchester Evening News
Oldham Chronicle
Preston Chronicle and Lancashire Advertiser
Reporter for the County Borough of Salford

Index